Nods and Becks

Nods and Becks

BY

FRANKLIN P. ADAMS

("F. P. A.")

Whittlesey House

McGRAW-HILL BOOK COMPANY, INC.

London   New York

NODS AND BECKS

Copyright, 1944, *by* FRANKLIN P. ADAMS

THIRD PRINTING

This book is produced in full compliance with the government's regulations for conserving paper and other essential materials.

PUBLISHED BY WHITTLESEY HOUSE
A division of the McGraw-Hill Book Company, Inc.

Printed in the United States of America

Haste thee, Nymph, and bring with thee
Jest and youthful Jollity,
Quips and Cranks and wanton Wiles,
Nods and Becks and wreathed Smiles.—*L'Allegro*.

ACKNOWLEDGMENTS

The author wishes to thank the following publications: The Atlantic Monthly, Good Housekeeping, Harper's Magazine, The Nation, The New York Herald Tribune, The New York Post, The New Republic, The New Yorker, The Saturday Evening Post, and The Saturday Review of Literature; also Doubleday, Doran & Company, Inc., for their permission to reprint.

Nods and Becks

BALLADE OF THE AMERICAN CRISIS

"These are the times that try men's souls."—Thomas Paine,
"The American Crisis," Dec. 23, 1776.

Echo again the words of Paine,
Clear as a mountain stream is clear,
Sane as a prairie breeze is sane.
Sound again on the listening ear
Critical words of another year.
Grandly, majestically, there rolls
Over the land, that all may hear:
"These are the times that try men's souls."

These are the days of stress and strain,
These are the nights of doubt and fear—
Fear of the love of earthly gain,
Doubt, that a wandering breath may veer.
Some of us swayed by the cynic's jeer,
Some unsure of a country's goals,
When life is cheap and living is dear,
These are the times that try men's souls.

One may work, though his work be vain,
To swell the chest of the profiteer;
One give his body and wealth and brain
To help his brothers, or far or near.
Ring, ye chimes of delight and cheer
As the bell of death and destruction tolls!
Smile, ye angels! Ye devils, leer!
These are the times that try men's souls.

ENVOY

Thou who whenever storms appear
Guidest us over the deeps and shoals,
Hold Thou the helm, and our Vessel steer!
These are the times that try men's souls.

INSIDE "INFORMATION, PLEASE!"

On a sunny afternoon in April, 1938, a solitary bus rider might have been seen wending his way northward. Our hero—for it was indeed I—debussed at 57th Street and proceeded to the office of Mr. John Moses, a radio agent.

A careful historian—again meaning me (Note: When the political columnists say "Every thinking man" they mean themselves, and when candidates appeal to "Every intelligent voter" they mean everybody who is going to vote for them)—records preceding chapters. For about six months, off and on, in the order named, I had been writing pieces and making auditions for the Columbia Broadcasting System, with conspicuous unsuccess. And one day my none too altruistic wife, having heard that Miss Dorothy Thompson had an agent who had got her engagements which it was reputed brought her income into the six-figure, or non-hay bracket, said, "I wish you'd meet this wonderful agent." A domestic pacifist, I am wax in the hands of the Little Woman's wish. So I went to Miss Thompson's for luncheon to meet the fabulous Mr. Moses, who interrupted Dorothy just long enough to tell me that he too was a Chicago boy who had attended the University of Michigan, and that if anything in my line came up he'd let me know. I didn't have a chance to tell him that I had no line. Also I had been a newspaperman for thirty-five years and I had heard a dozen city editors tell applicants that same old stuff about leaving name and address, and if anything came up, etc.—If any reporter or editorial writer ever got a job that way I shall be glad to publish his name, provided that a certain managing editor, who said he'd let me know when something in my line arose, furnishes me with a medium of printed expression. Hence the day upon which our story opens I was full of cynical doubt.

But that day Mr. John Moses telephoned me and invited me to his office.

"If this is no good," I said to him politely, "you'll have to pay my bus fare."

"Agreed!" he cried, "I want you to meet Dan Golenpaul."

I took the bus to 57th Street and there I met Mr. Golenpaul, who said that he would tell me what he had to say in a very few words.

"I doubt it," was my countercheck courteous.

"You've heard these quiz programs," he began. This being a declarative sentence, I was mute. Otherwise I'd have had to say no. "Well," he said, "I've got an idea to do a quiz program in reverse. The public sends in questions for a panel of experts—experts of whom you might be one."

"What questions?" I asked. "As for instance?"

"Well," he said, "who was the Merchant of Venice?"

"Antonio," I said.

"That's right," he said, obviously astonished at my omniscience. "Most people say Shylock."

"Not the people I am in the habit of associating with," I said, with utter and somewhat snobbish truth. So he asked me a few more straw dummies. And then I asked him a few, such as "What precedes 'and pastures new'? And how does 'The Old Oaken Bucket' begin?" Pretty near everybody, in pretty near anybody's set, says, "How dear to my heart" instead of "this heart." First thing we knew it was seven o'clock.

Now this game was Old Stuff to me. For years we had played this, or variations of it, at Herbert Bayard Swope's house parties—the host, Alexander Woollcott, Laurence Stallings, Arthur Krock, and I. And when Stanley Walker and I were co-slaves of the New York Herald Tribune we had

an agreement that either could call the other up at any time
of day, or night, and pose a question. Usually it was cog-
nominal, such as the names of Grayson M.-P. Murphy, and
what E. D. E. N. meant in Mrs. Southworth's name, and
what the D's were for—this was too easy—in John D. Rocke-
feller, Newton D. Baker, and Louis D. Brandeis. And the
e. e. in e. e. cummings and D. H. in Lawrence. The honey
though was knowing about Cyrus Hermann Kotzschmar
Curtis—I spelled Hermann with one *n*, which was worse in
our game than not knowing it at all.

In what seemed an incredibly short time after that first
meeting with Mr. Golenpaul he summoned me to an audition
on April 27, 1938. An audition is something like an entrance
examination. What you say is recorded on wax for the prying
ears of radio executives, as well as for the cannier ears of
possible sponsors. That night Mr. Fadiman, who was
almost as good at the start as he now is, fired queries at
Mr. Marcus Duffield, of the New York Herald Tribune;
Professor Harry Allen Overstreet, head of the philosophy
department at the College of the City of New York; Mr.
Louis Hacker, of the history department at Columbia University; Mr. Bernard Jaffe, author of "Crucibles" and
science teacher in Bushwick High School, Brooklyn. And me.
We made two auditions that night, one at 8:30 and one at
9:30. All that I remember about it is that I never expected
to hear any more about it.

And then we were told that on Tuesday, May 17th, we
were to be on the air. And the next Tuesday, the 24th, the
guest was Dr. Paul de Kruif, who didn't know that rubiola
was measles. It sounded to me like a tooth-wash, and I said
so, and people in the studio laughed at my honest endeavor
to disseminate information.

And on June 7th—a happy date for all concerned, especially for millions of his admiring listeners—John Kieran

became one of us, to put it mildly. And on July 5th Mr. Oscar Levant, composer, pianist, and Gershwinophile, became half of one of us, which is by way of saying that he appears on alternate broadcasts. So since that day we have one guest on Oscar's evenings, and two on the others.

The "Information, Please!" setup is its own and, compared with most other programs you may have heard, simple. The studio is small and if you ask why these places are called studios, it'll have to be a better etymologist than I to tell you. The best that Webster will do is to call a studio the workroom of a professional man; not the workroom—or with us, the playroom—of a lot of professional men, with spectators and auditors, to see and hear them work.

Still ours is comparatively a studio. The place seats two hundred and twenty, not counting us on the stage. There Mr. Clifton Fadiman exalted sits at a one-microphone table. At a table facing him, equipped with four microphones, sit the four of us. Every other week Mr. Oscar Levant, often described, but for the life of me I can't see why, as irrepressible, sits at the table's right, which is nearest the piano. Mr. Kieran is at his left, and the guest of the evening between Mr. Kieran and me. There is a silly and baseless notion that it is the part of wisdom to keep Mr. Levant and me as far apart as possible, but shucks! I wouldn't do him any physical harm—him in his early thirties. Besides, he needs his hands, for nobody plays that studio piano so well as he. I'd rather hear him play the piano than hear anybody I've ever heard. Many of my more musical friends ask why he might not play for the entire thirty minutes, which, especially if I got paid for listening, would delight me. Some of my non-musical friends ask me why he does anything but play, which is unfair, for Mr. Levant, in literature and sports and current matters, is not only a young man of wide knowledge, but also a fellow of exquisite taste in many things, and of another taste that makes even his idolaters wince at times. And I'll tell you why he is a great asset to "Information, Please!" He is unpredictable; there is a perhaps about him, which there is not, alas! about Kieran or me. A pair of veteran newspapermen, when we have nothing to say we say nothing, while Oscar is at his wordiest, and sometimes his best, under those conditions.

At Mr. Fadiman's right, so unobtrusively that he had been sitting there for more than a year of Tuesdays (remember those were the old unsponsored as well as the Canada Dry Ginger Ale days) before I was conscious of him, sits Our Founder, Mr. Dan Golenpaul. He checks the questions and gives Mr. Fadiman the statistics on how much our combined ignorance has cost, in war bonds and stamps and Encycs. Brit. per ig. And sitting somewhere behind us, except for the time when he vaunts our beloved sponsor, sits our announcer—once Mr. Milton Cross and now Mr. Ben Grauer.

For the first six months "Information, Please!" was unsponsored. The advertising boys told us—or told Mr. Golenpaul—that while of course they liked it, it was over the public's head; too highbrow. I never understood why so many persons—advertising executives and newspaper and magazine publishers—assume that the public is illiterate, or at any rate impervious to literacy. Let me hasten to add that when the Saturday Review of Literature gave us an award in 1940 "for Distinguished Service to Literature" I, for one, was frightened. It seemed pretentious; we weren't Literature's Distinguished Servants. We were men who were having a good time, and by a miracle, paid for having it. It happened that that same night we were similarly honored by the Hobo News, so we all felt better. Nor can I understand why we get awards for our educational value. What erudition is acquired by Mr. Kieran's telling a breathless

world that the 1912 World Series went to eight games, one
having been a tie, and that the Red Sox won because Fred
Snodgrass of the Giants muffed an easy fly? What educational value is in the fact that Judge James Garret Wallace
and I can sing the words and music of "She's More to Be
Pitied than Censured"? Of course I amass a not inconsider-
able amount of amazed knowledge from Mr. Christopher
Morley's mnemonic ability concerning every Sherlock
Holmes story ever written and from Mr. Deems Taylor's
merry memory of almost everything. Yet most of us recall
details and forget momentous matters. I think—and don't
you think I didn't have to look it up—of Thomas Bailey
Aldrich's "Memory":

> My mind lets go a thousand things,
> Like dates of wars and births of kings,
> And yet recalls the very hour—
> 'Twas noon by yonder village tower,
> And on the last blue noon in May—
> The wind came briskly up this way,
> Crisping the brook beside the road;
> Then, pausing here, set down its load
> Of pine-scents, and shook listlessly
> Two petals from that wild-rose tree.

And most of us, while we may forget the contents of this or
that schoolbook, can tell you that Swinton's Word Book
was light blue, and that Robinson's Arithmetic was maroon.

It is unlikely that anybody is ever going to send in a
question about the colors of my schoolbook covers, or that
anybody will ask me who sat in front of me in Miss Laura
E. Hull's room at Douglas School, Chicago. Yet similar
things, from childhood and youth, are not difficult to sum-
mon from the memory; they are merely unforgettable. And

that is why I am sincere when I pooh-pooh those who profess to be aghast at what they foolishly call feats of memory. When it comes to a few well-known poems, Mr. Kieran and I were introduced to poetry, we found by comparing early recollections, by the same book—Bryant's Library of Poetry and Song.

The choice of guests is wholly Entrepreneur Golenpaul's, and his selections are almost uniformly excellent. No field— medicine and architecture are the exceptions I can think of— is uncombed. Among our ablest and most enjoyable guests were Miss Gracie Allen and Mr. Fred Allen. Our most sweetly redolent guest, as well as the most orchidiferous, was Mrs. Osa Johnson. And there has been nobody whom we enjoyed more than Mr. Wendell L. Willkie. I recall somebody's astonishment at the fact that Mr. Willkie (he was on the air with us, and was the guest on one of our motion picture shorts, both before the 1940 convention) knew many things remote from law and the public utility business. I said that I thought it remarkable that anybody thought it remarkable that a university graduate (Indiana '13) should know or remember anything. "After all," said Mr. Willkie, "a fellow doesn't go through college blindfolded."

Upon what meat do these experts feed? Well, high-think, ing John Kieran is a plain liver; he never has a pre-broadcast morsel; Mr. Levant, before, during, and after dinner, has a few dozen cups of coffee; and I gorge, especially if I am Dan Golenpaul's invited or uninvited guest. Such a dinner is attended by our host, who just before and during a broadcast is as nervous as any Broadway Star on a first night; his wife, Ann, who is better looking than Dan (though her appearance merits greater praise than that); and the evening's program guest. These dinners are supposed to make the guest feel easy and comfortable, and sometimes they do.

During the ten minutes preceding the broadcast Mr. Fadiman, who in turn is preceded by our stage manager, who introduces Mr. Fadiman to the studio audience and toward the program's end, signifies digitally that there are two minutes left—explains to the studio audience that a few minutes will be devoted to sample questions and answers, the purpose being to comfort the guest and to assure him by demonstration of the friendly atmosphere that he is in. This warm-up period usually helps, for if the guest is unusually timorous he finds that the earth has not swallowed him up and that even ignorance of who is appearing in a current movie does not merit capital punishment. There is another thing that I find almost always true of our guests, especially of those who say, "I've never been so frightened in my life." At the end of the program when Mr. Fadiman says "That's all we'll have time for," the guests, like us so-called regulars, are astonished that the thing has ended so soon and wish that it might continue for another hour.

It seems to me that we have only one Indispensable— Mr. Clifton Fadiman. Excellent though listeners may consider him, nobody who has not sat across from him week after week can appreciate his marvelous sense of timing and what might be called his sweetly acid tolerance—his ability to silence us who are given to loquacity, and the sportsmanship of his wit are no sleeper-jump from genius. I am not guessing. For one evening, when he was poison-ivied to the point of silence, I substituted for him. I was unsuave and rattled, and though Danny ("Boy") Golenpaul was at my right hand to help me, I was no good. I went so fast that the only record I broke was in the number of questions asked. They told me that I had used sixteen questions (the average is eleven) and that I had forgotten to award one of the prizes. However, I achieved something that Mr. Fadiman never reached. Next day the World-Telegram headed the story "Adams Nervous as Quiz-Master." Beat that if you can, you ole Fadiman, you!

There have been various estimates of the number of questions "Information, Please!" receives. Doubtless the number varies from week to week. Considering that many questions have four parts, it adds up. The ultimate selection, after I don't know how many assistant editors go through them, is Our Boss's. Sometimes he picks a dull one, but his average is amazingly high. To me, at least, the ideal question is one that none of us answers, but makes us feel that we were saps not to have known that.

Often when we have a guest somebody erroneously thinks that the questions pointed at him or her are "fixed." No question is put which does not originate with the querist, although the precise wording may be amended. This is one way, for example, that questions up what Mr. Fadiman calls so-and-so's alley, come in: At the end of a broadcast Mr. Fadiman announces that our next week's guest will be, say, Sir Thomas Beecham or Miss Margaret Leech. That sends hundreds of hearers to the reference books, and during the week questions pour in about music or about Washington during the Civil War.

Of course there are one's friends who cannot see why their questions have not been used. They say:

1. I bet they don't read 'em.
2. Say, I sent in one that nobody could answer.
3. Why does Fadiman show his dislike to
   a. You
   b. Kieran (they usually call him Kernan)
   c. Levant?

Well, friends, listen:

1. They read 'em all.
2. There are thousands of such questions. One man told

me that he sent in "What was the population of
Saginaw, Mich., in 1910?" The program wouldn't be
any fun if it consisted of questions that neither we nor
our listeners could possibly answer. We have to be
given a sporting chance.
3. He doesn't show it. He hasn't it.

What these broadcasts evoke in the other boys I don't
know. After all, Fadiman, Kieran, and Levant are New
Yorkers, though Oscar was born, comparatively recently,
in Pittsburgh; but though thirty-eight years of incessant
daily writing may have caused somebody, once in a blue
lustrum, to say "That was a good piece you had in the
paper a few years ago; I forget what it was," the broadcasts, and the movie-shorts—which except for the fact that
some of the questions are visual, are just like the broadcasts—cause old friends to write to you and strangers to
accost you who never have read a single word of the millions
you have written. The injustice of it irritates me; I, a hard-
working writer, have been known to a few readers of whatever newspaper employed me. But what, if *I* may ask a
question, happens now? To a broadcast question I frequently
answer "I don't know." A man rushes up to me the next
morning and says, "I heard you on 'Information, Please!'
last night. You just slay me! You were marvelous." "Why,"
I say, "I don't remember saying anything but 'I don't
know.'" "That's just it," he says—no kidding, he *said* it—
"You say 'I don't know' as though it was the only thing
in the world you didn't know." Now what to do with such
hero worship?
Sometimes our actor-guests, accustomed as they are to
the immediate response of a large audience, say that they
have "mike fright," meaning that they grow self-conscious.
I can't speak for the other regulars, but it never occurs to

me that anybody but those of my sons who are allowed to stay up are listening. For next morning they say "Papa, you talk too much," or "Do you mean to say you didn't know that was from 'Macbeth'?"

One day a woman telephoned from New Canaan, Conn. She said that she was Mrs. Sherman Aldrich, and could she have a ticket to a broadcast. "I'm Bessie Knight," she added. Now at the ages from nine to twelve years I adored—but never told my love—the beautiful brown-eyed Bessie Knight, whose house I passed on my way to school in the hope—never realized—that she would emerge just as I was passing . . . and that broadcast night I looked about the studio, and I went up to the best-looking woman there and said, "Hello, Bessie!" . . . P. S. She said that she knew I had passed by her house.

And I have had letters from Miss Anna Wetter, who taught German to us in the sixth grade at Douglas School in the '90's.

And from an even earlier day came a letter from Louis Weinberg, of Weinberg Bros., who had the 35th Street butcher shop, with sawdust on the floor and a fountain in the window spraying the vegetables. Mr. Weinberg wrote, "Are you the Frankie Adams that used to come to market with your grandmother?" I am, and I did, and sometimes at the age of ten they would let me help drive the horse when the wagon delivered meat. And the next Thanksgiving he sent me the biggest turkey I've ever seen. . . . Doubtless the comparative tots, like Fadiman and Levant, get echoes from their kiddie-playmates of 1924.

Not to speak of a letter to me from a Captain, Q. M., who crossed on the Leviathan with me in March, 1918, and also crossed the Channel on the Londonderry from Southhampton to Le Havre's "rest" camp; and one from a man that gave me a harmonica with four keys in 1908.

There was the time that "Information, Please!" was sued for $17.62. I've never heard how the case came out. But one night, when Miss Alice Marble, fresh from winning the 1939 National Women's Singles Championship, was our excellent and personable guest—as, indeed had Mrs. Helen Wills Moody Roark been previously—the three men were adjured to shut their eyes and tell the colors of their neckties. Mine, I recall, was canary. Well, that night as Mr. James J. Behr was driving through Boston, Mass., with his radio turned on, he heard that query. He also closed his eyes, hit the car ahead of him, and paid $17.62 for fender damage. Cheap life insurance, at that.

You'll have to excuse me. It's nearly half-past nine, Eastern War Time. Time to wake up, America, and stump the experts. Experts, my grandmother's left hind hat!

* * *

MONOTONY

Day after day, night after night,
My life at home is far from bright;
But even home has more variety
Than I find in café society.

* * *

ON THE INEPTITUDE OF A SIMILE OF COLERIDGE'S

And listens like a three years' child.—"The Rime of the Ancient Mariner."

Coleridge! thou shouldst be living at this hour:
Thou in thy tomb a century or more
(To be precise, d. 1834)
How impotent thy pen, thy simile how sour!
How nil thy knowledge of the articulate power
Of infants! Little, alas, thy lore
Of modern parentage, or of the chore
Of modern children and their verbal shower!

"And listens like a three years' child." O say
  Not ever of a little child at all
  From sun his rise till after night her fall
That he doth listen; nor let any sing
Of listening like a child. O triply nay!
  It is we parents do the listening.

*　*　*

(*The short paragraphs that follow appeared in The Conning
Tower 1921–1922*)

Another promise we make is that, if elected mayor, we
never shall write a letter or issue what is known as a Statement, beginning "My attention has been called."

Nor shall we ever employ the cost-nothing and patronizing
brand of flattery. It is common with politicians. It is the kind
that, if used in the preceding paragraph, would have made
it read: "If elected mayor of this great city."

It is the kind of locution used by a candidate, when he
says, "I intend to give the thinking voters an opportunity
to protest." Designedly or unconsciously, that is supposed
to make the non-thinking voter think he is a thinking voter.
If a man dependent on public favor, which is to say votes,
had to rely on the thinking anybodies, he might as well
decide to End It All. It's the non-thinking lads that our
appeal, if any, is made to.

*　*　*

Our notion of an optimist is a man who, knowing that
each year was worse than the preceding, thinks next year
will be better.

And a pessimist is a man who knows the next year can't
be any worse than the last one.

*　*　*

"In something over five decades," philosophizes our favorite Marion, Ohio, newspaper, the Star, "we fail to recall where anybody ever boosted his own business or that of his community by dwelling on business depression." In something more than five minutes, which is a long time to give any subject, we fail to recall one instance of anybody starting a business boom by playing a piccolo solo in a graveyard.

* * *

When Keats was twenty-three years of age he said he had "little knowledge and middling intellect." "It is true," he wrote, "that in the height of enthusiasm I have been cheated into some fine passages" (and that, to our notion, is one of them); "but that is not the thing." Also he thought that if he should die, he would leave no immortal work behind him—nothing to make his friends proud of his memory; "but if I had time I would have made myself remembered." Probably time would not have added anything to Keats. We have ceased to fool ourself about time, environment, tranquillity, or climate. We never used to see a large clean desk in a quiet room that we didn't think, "If I only could work under such conditions, I might Put it Over." But we know now that there is no Synthetic Afflatus.

* * *

Old Don Marquis and young Professor Heywood Broun have been printing their animadversions upon Age and Achievement. As readers of this Eiffel of Emptiness never miss a line written by these broad-visioned and -shouldered gentlemen, it is unnecessary to republish what they said. Both, in a word, thought that some day, when they were older, they would do the Big Stuff. Well, we recovered our thoughts *De Senectute* years ago, when Marquis and Broun were young and gracile, or ever Ambition had picked at the counterpane.

There is a time (we think we said) when you say to yourself: "This isn't good, but it isn't bad for a kid. At thirty perhaps I'll have something to say, and even if I haven't, I'll know how to say nothing supremely well." Then—many years elapsing while you still make excuses to yourself, on the ground of youth, for your ineptitude—you look at the old stuff you did long years ago, and say: "Why can't I do as well as that now?" . . . And the truth probably is that the early stuff was bad because it was unripe, and the late stuff is bad because you haven't anything to say, and never will have anything to say. . . . Ho! hum! this snow is likely to make the tennis season late.

* * *

BALLADE OF A SHORT FELT WANT

Washington's life full well I know,
From the Parson Weems to the Rupert Hughes;
How he crossed the Delaware's ice and snow—
I know that painting, its buffs and blues.
Lives of the Adamses—J.'s, J. Q.'s,
Sam's, and soon they'll probably spill more.
Where is biography's nose for news?
Why don't they write about Millard Fillmore?

Dozens and dozens the Lives of Poe;
I've seen one of Chauncey M. Depew's;
Everyone's written of Hank Thoreau;
There's even a book about Henry Clews;
Lives of the Barrymores and the Drews;
Life of the bandmaster, Patrick Gilmore,
Come from the presses—don't ask me whose.
Why don't they write about Millard Fillmore?

— 17 —

The Jeffersons, Tom and the actor Joe;
George A. Custer and all the Sioux;
Now there's a Life of E. P. Roe;
And "Andrew Johnson" got swell reviews;
Benjamin Franklin without his shoes;
Teddy and Franklin—and few themes thrill more.
But—against Millard are there taboos?
Why don't they write about Millard Fillmore?

L'ENVOI

Biographers looking for themes to choose
More of the same things write, and still more.
Why don't they write what I'd fain peruse?
Why don't they write about Millard Fillmore?

* * *

I KNOW ALMOST EVERYTHING

It happens that I know almost everything, and one of the
things that I know is that it just happens; it is chance, and
chance alone. You know how it is. You are looking up a
definition, or a quotation. What definition? What quotation? I was looking up a word that I had come across in
reading,—I always stop when I strike an unfamiliar word,—
and the word was *nubility*. I found that it meant marriage-
ability, but that *nubilation* meant cloudiness. So I remembered from way back in First Year Latin that *nubes, nubis*
was a cloud, and that *nubility* came from *nubo*, the verb
from whose participle *nuptial* is derived. So, as the fellow
says, what? Not only useless information, but also dull.

And once I was looking up to prove that it was Isaac
Watts and not Reginald Heber who wrote "Little drops of
water." And that was the time that I came across "Onward,
Christian Soldiers," whose music I knew was Arthur Sullivan's, but whose words, I then found out never to forget,

were S. Baring-Gould's. Better than that, S. for Sabine. Not that these facts, found by accident, are momentous to me. But most of the other things I know have stuck because I am easily diverted from the main search. Not that I am alone. Columbus was looking for India; Hudson for China. Nor did Marconi have an idea that he was going to be responsible for Jack Benny or "Information, Please!"—bless his (Marconi's) heart! If it didn't take so much research, I'd like to write a piece called "By-products of Research," for I have a notion that many of the discoveries, inventions, stories, poems, and even paintings, have been come upon because the creator was trying to do something else.

I know hundreds of poems, if not all the way through, at least the first few lines. On the library table when the table and I were about ten years of age, there was a copy of Bryant's *Library of Poetry and Song*. There were subdivisions, such as Poems of Love, Poems of Places, and Humorous and Satirical. It was this that I liked and read first, though why they should put the best poems last I couldn't see.

I never committed anything to memory, but some poems I have read so often that I know them by heart. I think that the first poem that I read was Bret Harte's "Plain Language from Truthful James." And years later, when I was reading Swinburne, I found that

> Which I wish to remark—
>   And my language is plain—
> That for ways that are dark
>   And for tricks that are vain,
> The Heathen Chinee is peculiar:
>   Which the same I would rise to explain.

is the same as "Hertha" and that Bret Harte was putting his poem into

Have I set such a star
To show light on thy brow
That thou sawest from afar
What I show to thee now?
Have ye spoken as brethren together,
   the sun and the mountains and thou?

And I think what mischievous fun Bret Harte must have had when he burlesqued "Man, equal and one with me, man that is made of me, man that is I," with "Yet he played it that day upon William and me in a way I despise."

It is worthless knowledge; it helps nobody; it never did me any good; it'll never help me; and I can't ever forget it. I know hundreds of irrelevant and equally useless things. I have been at newspaper writing for forty years. I know it is Rea Irvin and Irving Berlin and Ervin Wardman and Irvin Cobb and Will Irwin and Hervey Allen. I know that my teachers in Douglas School, Chicago, were Miss Werkmeister, Miss Emily Freiberger, Mrs. Dreyfus, Mrs. Lester, Mrs. Kewley, Miss Pierce, Miss Shoemaker, Mrs. Swarthout, and, best of all, Miss Ellen M. Stowe. At graduation we sang "The Landing of the Pilgrim Fathers." Speaking of songs, I remember "The Daughter of Officer Porter" because it was sung in 1896 by Lady Sholto Douglas who wore a diamond garter and skirts that showed her knees.

The first complete book I read was *Davy and the Goblin*, a book inspired by *Alice*. Yet I never considered Lewis Carroll comparable to Charles Edward Carryl, who wrote *Davy*, which had "A capital ship for an ocean trip" and "The night was thick and hazy When the *Piccadilly Daisy*." Oh, I can go through both of them from memory.

I know many a mathematical formula, and could still arrive at one or two. The only one that I use is the one for arithmetical progression. And that only in rotation pool, as the balls are numbered from 1 to 15. Well, s the sum, n the number, a the first number, and l the last.

$$s = \frac{n(a + l)}{2}$$

Then

$$s = \frac{15(1 + 15)}{2}$$

$$s = \frac{240}{2} = 120$$

So you know that you have to get 61 points to win.

I know a lot of Latin; and most of it I learned after I left school, though I had a good foundation. But for many years I had a newspaper column to fill, and I had read that Eugene Field, whom all Chicago boys revered, filled his "Sharps and Flats" with translations of Horace. So I did some. And it was fun, though it often took the best part of two days to do eight satisfactory lines, which doesn't plug much of a columnar gap.

But this I know: what you learn when you're not trying to learn, when your mind is relaxed, is likely to stick. Years ago I heard somebody say, "'Twas ever thus, from childhood's happy hour." People still say it, and I scream. I knew that was wrong, because "happy" made two extra syllables, yet I looked it up. Of course I found that it was "Oh! ever thus." So I ran a series of Familiar Misquotations, such as "Shall fold their tents like the Arabs, And silently steal away," when it should be "*as* silently." So I developed a passion for accuracy, mostly because I always have hated sloppiness; I hate the person who, because he doesn't know that the day Fred Merkle didn't touch second was September 23, 1908, says, "What difference does it make?" None. You may be ignorant of most facts, and careless, and wise; you may have great knowledge and accuracy, and no wisdom. But oftener knowledge and wisdom, in varying degree, are in the same person. As the late Hugh E. Keough said,—I quote him often, and accurately, too,—"The race is not always to the swift, but that is where to look."

I am a little ashamed when during a broadcast of "Information, Please!" I am able to sing, or recite, the words of some song that was popular in 1897. Well, in those days I went at least once a week to the variety shows then current. Songs lasted longer than they do now; and there was sheet music that everybody had, and nearly everybody played, instead of taking music vicariously on the radio. There were ballads that told stories, and no silly "Hutsut" something or other. Who could help remembering "Just Tell Them That You Saw Me" when it had lines like "'Is that you, Madge?' I said to her. She quickly turned away"?

There seems to be mild astonishment that I should know many of the words and most of the music in the Gilbert and Sullivan operettas. In my childhood my father played many of the melodies, and in 1934, when the D'Oyly Carte Opera Company toured the United States, I heard each of them many times. You don't forget things that you like.

John Kieran was telling some boys at the Gunnery School, Washington, Connecticut, how he knew such a lot about art. "I covered big league baseball for eighteen years," he said. "Ballplayers and baseball writers are lazy. They don't do anything till it's time for the game. I had nothing to do all morning, so I went to the art galleries. There's at least one in every big league town. You can't help sopping up a lot of admiration for certain paintings, and then you want to know about the painters." And he learned French literature by failing to waste two hours a day on the subway for over a year.

Remembering something of what I learned at school makes me a hero to my children. I can explain the solution of a quadratic equation to one, and the ablative absolute to another. *Can?* I do.

And yet there are things that I don't know, and expect never to know. I don't know why I can't get crisp bacon, strong coffee, or rare beef. No cook believes me. Cooks appear to think that I can't possibly like it the way they don't. I don't know why a wife says, "Hurry, we're due at Rodgers's in ten minutes. *I'm* all ready," and you shave, take a bath, and dress, and still she isn't ready. I don't know what women do between the times that they are ready and are ready. Or why women hate to be at a station more than a few seconds before train time. I don't know why anybody of any sex says, "I don't get time to read," except that such people simply dislike reading. For everybody throws away at least one hour a day. I don't know why anybody who has lived in the United States thinks of Hitler as he might think of an unpleasant fellow, and why he doesn't know that the Hitlerian ambition is so ruthless and cruel that there are still millions of us who can't yet take in an idea so foreign to anything in our experience. I read about divorce, and I can't see why two people can't get along together in harmony, and I see two people and I can't see how either of them can live with the other. I don't know why I read so many things—books and magazine and newspaper pieces—written by those who know more about everything than I do about anything. I don't know who, if not I, first said that—about whom.

I don't understand the principle of the radio. Nor for that matter the telephone or the telegraph. Don't explain it to me; I don't get it.

I don't know why people tidy up my desk so that I can't find anything. I don't know why I don't slap the next person who asks me, "What's the use of voting?" I don't know why some stores or restaurants keep a loud radio going all the time. "Did anybody request this?" I ask. "Request what?" "That the radio be turned on." "Why, no," says the proprietor. "Well, I request that it be turned off." "Sure," he says, surprised that there was any noise. I don't know why employers won't pay those who work for them anything they ask, or why workers don't believe that employers pay them enough. Why, I always have been overpaid, while I grind down the few employees I have had—and no longer can afford.

I don't know why people, especially in war work, don't realize that if nobody cared who got the credit for this or that, as long as the objective were gained, red tape would fade to a mild pink, and the output would at least double in quantity and increase in quality. This doesn't go for peacetime or inspirational work. How many, for example, know who wrote that famous poem, "Tinker to Evers to Chance"? . . . I wrote it.

* * *

A CONNECTICUT LAD

I

The bells they sound for broadcast,
    But friends have gone away
To glean the gold that they may hold
    A harvest far from hay.

Up Kellogg's Hill to Easton,
    Past Harrington's and Wing's,
The pilgrims come and see the home
    Of Mr. Raymond Swing's.

And who shall jog to Georgetown
    And bear the boreal brunts

May see the fair and lovely lair
    Of Mr. Frazier Hunt's.

Down Steep Hill Road from Good Hill
    The farer from afar
No song may hear, but see anear
    Mr. James Melton's car.

II

For guerdon at the Garden
    The boxers at their fights
Are watched by people paying
    To stay from home o' nights.

But afternoons in Weston,
    For money not at all,
We see the Hurlbutt schoolboys
    Get beat at basket ball.

III

When snow comes down in Stepney,
    And ice is Easton Road,
I read beside the fire
    Blazing in my abode.

On hills too high for skiing
    The noisy children speed
So merry and so mirthful
    I can no longer read.

IV

The sun is growing stronger,
    And later lingers day,
And afternoons are longer—
    As only fools gainsay.

In Meriden and Moosup,
  As briefer grows the night
It seems we use less juice up,
  Says the bill for electric light.

* * *

Utterly selfish is our hope that the movies continue to be called a menace. For the folks who used to talk about the Curse of Rum now talk about the Menace of the Movies. And when the censorship board takes the Sin out of the Cinema, there will be the newspapers to blame for the woes of the world. . . . The world, although some of our best friends are resident members of it, reminds us of the hangover who says, "I should never have eaten those soft-boiled eggs last week."

* * *

As we see censorship it is a stupid giant traffic policeman answering "Yes" to "Am I my brother's copper?" He guards a one-way street and his semaphore has four signs, all marked "STOP."

* * *

"Well," said the office cynic, as he read that Mrs. Bourasse had received a present of a $26 bottle of perfume from Mr. Swarts and that she, in return, had bought him a pair of gold cuff links for $10, "she had a fairer sense of exchange than most of 'em."

* * *

Many a novel has sprung full-armed from an author's brain-waves with less than the following personal, from the Butte *Miner:* "Will the gentleman who picked up a lady who fell Tuesday morning on E. Granite St. by Hennessy's store please call at 17 E. Summit St.?"

* * *

One who lives adjacent to a Philadelphia school tells us that the children sing songs like "The Love Nest" in the classroom, which recalls the first song we were forced—by Miss Werkmeister, Room 22, Douglas School—to sing. It was something like:

> In all the green world there is none so sweet
> As my little lamb with its nimble feet;
> His eyes are so bright, his wool so white;
> O, he is my darling, my heart's delight!

But our favorite that year was:

> Where do all the daisies go?
> *I* know, *I* know.
> Underneath the snow they creep;
> Nod their little heads and sleep;
> In the Springtime out they peep—
> That is where they go.
> In the Springtime out they peep—
> That is where they go.

What worried us the first day of school was how everybody but us in the room appeared to know the words and music of these songs. Was the world, we thought, frightened to dizziness, like that? Was everybody to know more than we? And that, Dr. Freud, is a fear we never have been able to overwhelm. . . . The other children, we learned later, knew these songs because their older brothers and sisters had sung them.

And yet it wasn't long after that first day that a youth named Hosmer Dorland and we were kept in after school for having sung too loud.

* * *

HORACE ON THE CAMPAIGN

"Integer vitae, scelerisque purus_____".—

Horace: Book I, Ode 22.

He who is upright in his way of living,
Honest and fair, needs never the protection
Wisecracks or whisperings or poisoned phrases,
        Voter, can give him.

Whether his campaign be in California,
Maine or Alaska, Michigan or Utah,
Or through the valley bordered by the famous
        Father of Waters.

Once in the Weston woods, as I was walking
Near Lyons Plain, unarmed and free of worry,
Singing of Roosevelt, a vicious wolf that heard me
        Came up; and left me.

Monstrous and mad this terrorizing lupine,
Not such as you might look for in the Daunian
Forest of oaks, or in the Juban desert—
        No, he was viler.

Place me, a voter, on the Appalachians,
Stick me in Cleveland, Owosso, or Chicago,
Route me to Butte or send me to Seattle,
        Akron or Boston—

Yes, if you send me far across the oceans,
Anywhere at all within the solar system,
Still will I shout the universal name of
        Franklin D. Roosevelt.

* * *

What sort of place would the world be—and there, Mr. H. G. Wells, is a subject fit to your hand—if writers of every kind should disarm, for, say, ten years? All publications to discontinue; all writers to throw away pencils, pens, and typewriters.

Of course it is interesting—for about a minute, which is as long as most of us can endure sustained thinking—to speculate as to what the world would be like under those conditions; but what interests us even more is an answer to What Sort of Place Is It Now?

* * *

"Men," says Mr. W. L. George, "never ask women to talk about themselves." Which, if true, shows a high degree of efficiency.

But it isn't true. They do ask women to talk about themselves. And women ask men to talk about themselves. Many an entangling alliance has been formed with nothing to begin with but "Now tell me about yourself."

Women, our observation has been, listen more sedulously to men's recitals of self than men do to women's. Possibly that is so because women—by training, necessity, or general love of approbation—are Pleasers. . . . We often wonder how many million women a day listen, or pretend to listen, to epics whose burden is, "And I says to the boss, 'Looka here, who do you think you're talkin' to?"

* * *

Speaking, as we recently were, of advertising ideas we never were able to sell, years ago, fascinated by "Barking Dog Tobacco—It Never Bites," we offered slogans to other concerns, without success. Most of them we cannot recall, but there were:

Just-Before-Dawn Shoe Polish—It's Darkest.
Burnt-Child-Gasoline—It Dreads the Fire.

Time-and-Tide Elevators—They Wait for No Man.
Douglas Steaks—Tender and True.

* * *

It is a malicious pleasure to think, riding up in the cool Subway, of the motorists driving home through traffic jams; and it is a malicious pleasure to muse, driving home through the fresh air, of the thousands standing up in the hot and sticky Subway.

* * *

PSYCHOANALYSIS FOR THE KIDDIES

I. "Georgie Porgie, pudding and pie"

Case 4671—Georgie P____ came to my office, much perturbed. The patient had disturbing dreams, recurrent, to the effect that he saw his mother in various unfavorable circumstances—poverty, dishonor, violent death, remarriage. It was as plain a case of mother fixation as I ever treated.

I discovered that his mother, an excellent cook of meat and vegetables, was a poor hand at pastry—conspicuously poor. This gave Georgie P____ an inordinate desire for pudding and pie, and served to increase his hatred for his mother, for she deprived him of the food he liked, adoration of which became a consuming obsession. I considered it significant that his matrophobia was so pronounced that he tried to get the name, Mother Goose, changed, fearing lest his mother think that the anserine appellation was his own idea.

After 418 one-hour visits, I managed to learn that his fear and hatred of his mother caused him to kiss the girls; that when the girls came out to play, George P____ fled in terror, rather than listen to another output of feminine tears.

The patient was induced to experiment less miscellaneously, the promiscuity-desire being another protest against the undoubted virtue of his mother, who, obviously, often had made him cry. After another year of daily treatment, he attempted, his unconscious now unsuppressed, to kiss only one girl. This was attended with success, and a pleasurable sensation. He kissed her repeatedly, and, as she failed to exhibit any hysteria or infantilism that resulted in audible or visible lacrimosity, he concentrated on this woman, the consequence of which was monogamy, and a complete cure.

* * *

There are, according to recently published figures, 10,000,-000 feeble-minded persons in the United States. And there isn't a magazine or newspaper circulation manager in the country that doesn't get a secret thrill out of that statistic.

* * *

. . . He seemed to feel that, like the Caucasian in the jingle, the native American stock was "played out."—*The Freeman*

That jingle of Bret Harte's was written in the sonorous and dignified meter of Swinburne's "Atalanta in Calydon." What does the *Freeman* ask of a poet to graduate him from the jingle school?

Calling anything that isn't a ponderous piece of prosody a jingle is as typical of the reviewer's attitude as it is revelatory. Humorous verse, light verse, must be referred to as jingles, or "amusing of its kind," or "good of its sort."

What this sort of critic says to himself when he consciously—or otherwise—patronizes humorous writing is, "Anybody, including, of course, myself, who wanted to take a few seconds off some afternoon could write light and humorous stuff."

* * *

Our notion of a careful investigator is a man who verifies the declaration, printed after the name of a notary public, "My commission expires March 30, 1945."

* * *

Ours is a sincere doubt as to whether the question "And what did *you* do during the Great War?" might not embarass, among others, God.

* * *

BREAD-AND-BUTTER LETTERS

Your country-house guest room
Is never your best room.

Varying inversely as the excellence of their cooks
Is the number of all hostesses' books.

Next time I'll bring my own supply;
My host's cigars are too damned dry.

No matter how frequently I beg,
They won't give me a soft-boiled egg.

Why do all hostesses, the meanies,
Never serve cocktails but Martinis?

To me opaquer than is Greek
Is why their coffee's always weak.

When sunrise comes at 5:15,
Why yellow shades instead of green?

This is another I don't know:
Why, bidden, do I always go?

* * *

REMEMBER THE DAY

There is a superstition abroad that men, immersed in More Important affairs, forget their wives' birthdays and wedding anniversaries. Most ancient of wheezes is that one about the Little Woman's asking the Crabbed Old Gentleman coyly, sentimentally: "Dear, do you know what Day this is?"

Whereat he says, looking up from the evening paper (*Note:* my hypothetical men always look up from the evening paper. I would be glad to tell what paper he looks up from, if properly approached): "Sure, it's Wednesday."

Well, she does one of two things. She bursts into tears or she upbraids him for a monster. Why, years ago, in what used to be known as courting days, he remembered not only her birthday, but also the day they met, the first time he kissed her (not that these two didn't occur simultaneously sometimes, if memory serves), and their wedding day.

How it is in other families, I don't know. I live in the country, and what with gasoline shortages and one thing and another, I don't get around much. As a corollary, people can't come to see us, which is something of a masked blessing. Because people who come to see you always stay too long. In those days-beyond-recall when a twenty-mile drive for dinner was nothing, you could go over to Ross's or Chase's, and, if you wanted to, or you both wanted to, you left early. But either we have chairs equipped with glue or I am a magnetic host. Because when we used to have visitors, they dug in. First thing they knew, it was midnight. *I* knew it. I thought it was much later. "Goodness," said the visitors, "I had no idea it was so late." Now where was I? Oh, yes—I don't get around much, so I don't know how it is with other families.

But as I was saying, the idea that men don't remember is a superstition, a cliché, an axiom, a bromidiom, a silly notion, which, if it weren't for, I would never have been asked to write this piece.

Well, take my wife, if you know what I mean, and if you don't know, you're a snake in the grass. Take my wife, for example. So what? So we first met at a New Year's party and did not see each other again until Saturday night, February 10, the same night that *Icebound* (and don't tell me it is a coincidence that I remember this, because *Icebound* received the Pulitzer Award that year) opened. Our wedding day was May 9, 1925.

Anthony Adams was born on November 19, 1926; Timothy Adams on April 18, 1928; Persephone Adams on July 20, 1931; and Jonathan Adams on December 3, 1932. Their mother's birthday is June 4, and I won't tell you what year, you cad! My secretary, Martha Clave, and Edna St. Vincent Millay have February 22 for their natal day, which seems to be a good day for being born.

Now, I remember these birthdays and other anniversaries with ease, though materially I commemorate them with difficulty, if any. The Washington Birthday girls are simply mnemonics. Tim, my second son, born on the 18th of April, wasn't named Paul Revere only because Ma probably hadn't read any Longfellow since her Hawthorne schooldays. Even now, though she spends every summer a few miles from Brunswick, Maine, she (a woman) doesn't remember that Longfellow and Hawthorne were classmates (1825) at Bowdoin. However, she remembers our wedding day and her birthday quite well.

About three years ago my oldest boy was reading Carl Sandburg's *The War Years*. "When did Lincoln deliver the Gettysburg Address?" he asked me. I said, "1863." He said, "Yop, and on my birthday."

So next day, *credite aux non*, a man named, for argument's sake, Clifton Fadiman, asked me on a radio program, "What was the date of Lincoln's Gettysburg Address?"

"November 19, 1863," was my immediate response.

"However did you know that?" he asked me.

"I have a son who was born on that day," I said, "but not, on second thought, in 1863."

I added, thinking of Tim's Paul Revere birthday, "I have boys born on many commemorative days."

"More power to you," said good-natured Mr. F.

And such is the sensitivity of the listening millions that many letters were received objecting to the Fadiman "indelicacy."

"Women and elephants," observed Dorothy Parker in the refrain of a ballade, "never forget." My family, at the moment of writing, is unfortunately elephantless, so I can't say. But my birthday, which is also the birthday of Mr. Justice Felix Frankfurter, Mr. Vincent Astor, and Mr. W. Averell Harriman, occurs on November 15. So, on the morning of my recentest birthday, I had breakfast with two of my children, who are still at home. And the kids, who were at breakfast, far from singing *Happy Birthday to You*, didn't even say "Good-morning" to their old father. This includes Persephone, a woman-to-be.

Memento diem! This stuff about men who are so immersed in work that they haven't time to remember this day or that day is Grade-A Bunk. It's the women—the women who can't remember what they did with the ignition key, when the ration coupons expire, or to enter payments or deposits in a checkbook. They can't remember *when* they've had time to read. Nor can they remember when they had a winter like this one! Or what they did with the fountain pen you let them take. It's the women, who are like that Tall Blonde in the George Ade fable, "Who knew what cold cream to use and that Columbus discovered America and let it go at that. . . ."

Men remember the day. And the month. AND the year!

* * *

AUTUMNAL REVERIE

The maple trees are crimson;
The maple trees are gold.
know a weed called Jimson;
The weather's turning cold.

The cellar sings of cider;
The fodder's in the shock.
There is a duck called eider,
And an island known as Block.

The frost begins to tingle;
The kine are in the byre.
Oh, sweet the cosy ingle
Where roars the blazing fire.

My love is lush and mellow,
And alien she to grief,
Though life is sere and yellow
As any autumn leaf.

And whosoe'er excurses
Throughout the Nature Cult
Of regular autumn verses
Will get the same result.

* * *

SAYING IT WITH FLOWERS

I am not of the patronizing sort that doesn't read—or
affects not to read—the boxing news, the Gossip of Film-
land, the Frank Crane stuff, the syndicated "How to Keep
Well" articles. I read them all and they do me good, for I
take them seriously. In fact, I owe my clean-limbed young

Americanism chiefly to my adherence to advice that I read
a few years ago in "The Life of Jess Willard." Mr. Willard
advised me—I always think the author is looking straight
at me—to do certain exercises daily, and every day since
the morning I read that counsel I have done those strength-
ening exercises. Somebody told me, a few days after I began
to emulate Mr. Willard, that Mr. Willard didn't write those
pieces at all, but that they were written by Mr. George
Creel. It was like telling me there was no Santa Claus. I
think I cried a little, but I kept right on with the exercises,
and now anybody that says a word against George Creel
has me, with five or six years of unremitting training, to fight.

I take, as I said, the printed word seriously. A dealer
myself in the printed word, it never occurs to me that anyone
might read my own carefully chiseled phrases and say, "Yes,
but is it true?" or, "Oh, well, I doubt it," or even, "What
of it?"

I am like Ernest in the old Ade fable, who had been
Kicked in the Head by a Mule when young and Believed
everything he Read in the Sunday Papers.

And so this evening—my passion for truth makes me
refrain from saying the other day, because it wasn't the
other day, though it will be when this appears—I read,
among other things on the woman's page (and what I started
out to say was that I am not of the patronizing sort that
pretends not to read the woman's page) an "article," as
they call them, by Dorothy Dix. It was entitled, "Do
Woman Want to Be Petted?" and, with my habit of answering every question, rhetorical or not, that is put to me, I
said, "No," and added, with a revealing candor that I use
in meditation, "at any rate, not by me."

Well, I read this piece of Miss Dix's, which told of the
sufferings and sacrifices of the average married woman. "The
only thing that can repay her," I read, as I stood in the

warm, well-lighted subway train, speeding along through the night, after a jolly day spent in the joys of literary composition in a room full of reporter-pounded typewriters and thrillingly noisy telegraph instruments, "is the tenderness of her husband. His kisses, warm with love, and not a chill peck of duty on the cheek, his murmured words of endearment, are the magic coin that settles the long score that a woman charges up against matrimony, and that makes her rich in happiness."

"The woman"—by this time the train had got to Fourteenth Street, and the crowd of eager, merry homegoers, ardent to arrive at their joyous apartments, made reading difficult—"who has looked from the lovely gown and soft furs in a show window to her own shabby frock, and known that she could afford nothing better because the children had to have shoes and the coal was nearly out; the woman who has wrestled with pots and pans and the wash tub all day, while the baby howled and the other children fought, until her nerves were raw—will she be soothed by her husband's treating her as an equal when he comes home at night, and conversing with her about the Federal Reserve bank and the railroad situation? I trow not."

"But if"—and this took me from Seventy-second Street to Cathedral Parkway—"he puts his arms about her, and pats her on the shoulder, and says, 'There, there, now,' and tells her she is the dearest, bravest, most wonderful little woman in the world, and he just wishes he had the money to doll her up and show people that his little wifekins has got any of those living pictures backed off the screen, why, somehow, the tiredness goes out of her back, and the envy out of her soul, and the sun's come again in her heaven, and she is ready to go down on her knees and thank God for giving her such a husband, even if he isn't a money maker."

I emerged from the subway, and soft and glowing with

the romance Miss Dix had suffused me with, I stopped at a florist's. "How much," I asked, "are those violets?" "Two dollars," he said, as who should say, "And what a privilege to buy them at any price!" "I send them?" "No," I said. He wrapped them with the contemptuous air florists have for men who carry their offerings with them. They, I take it, are the transient trade. Your real wooer, it came over me in a flash, never brings his flowers.

I entered the house with the airy tread of youth, adventurous and confident. The Little Woman, as I call her in my lighter moments, was seated at her desk writing checks—struggling, I mused, with the problem of inelastic currency.

"See," I said, pointing with modest triumph to the violets.

"Where did you get them?" she asked.

"At Papakopolos's," I said.

"Well," she said—and I have no doubt she was right—"if you paid more than a dollar you got stuck. You always let a florist give you anything. Go and put them in the ice box."

"There, there, now," I said, quoting Miss Dix. "You are the dearest, bravest, most wonderful little woman in the world. I just wish I had the money to doll you up and show people that my little wifekins has got any of those living pictures backed off the screen."

"Since when," asked the Little Woman—and she is the bravest, as Miss Dix says, l. w. in the world—"since when have living pictures gone into the movies, and is that where you go in the afternoon when I call the office at three and they say you've left for the day? No wonder you never make any money. . . . Do you know why Wabash Preferred A and those other railroad stocks don't go up? It's partly because of the full-crew law and partly because of the Federal Reserve Board."

Well, she had me there. I don't know much about the Federal Reserve, and my whole interest in the railroad situation is in whether a train I am on or am waiting for is on time or late.

I get about a good deal, looking for what my admirers call Material for my Little Articles, and I meet lots of people. If I ever meet Miss Dix, I am going to introduce her to the Little Woman.

* * *

There are seventy stanzas in the Uruguay national anthem, which fact may account for the Uruguay standing army.

* * *

"Why in hell don't you keep still?" Mr. Charles W. Morse is quoted by The World as having said to newspapermen who asked him whether he had anything to say about the government's investigation of his shipbuilding for it. Whether any newspaperman replied to Mr. Morse's query the record fails to state, but one answer might have been to the effect that it is the newspaperman's job, as a public servant, to print the news; and that he couldn't get the news by keeping still.

Also it occurs to us that the newspaperman meets only two classes: Those who want to know why he printed it and those who want to know why he didn't. And in the course of years the newspaperman, who in an effort at honesty, prints many things and omits printing many things, loses many friendships—friendships insecurely founded, perhaps, but friendships whose wabbly foundations seem safe until they crumble. Our advice to young men about to enter journalism is to enter it if possible, for any other business or profession seems to us like shooting craps for no stakes. But to the youth we should add: "Any friends you must consider as so much velvet."

* * *

"SPARKS OF LAUGHTER NO. 2"

Stewart Anderson, Inc.

Readers and friends—and I hope that those words are as interchangeable as words were the night of the dinner party when the young lady was sitting next to the Bishop of X. It seems it was the first time she had been quite so close to such a dignitary, and her tongue was paralyzed. The silence between them became more and more embarrassing to her. At length some fruit was passed, and she snatched at the opportunity to open a conversation, and said, "Are you very fond of bananas?" The dear old prelate, a trifle deaf, thought she said "pyjamas," and after thinking for a moment, chin on hand, he answered, "My dear young lady, since you have asked me I will frankly state that I much prefer the old-fashioned nightshirt."

But seriously, dear readers, I am proud and pleased to have as my theme this morning a book that needs, if I may be allowed to say so, not my weak praise to place it among the most enjoyable books of the year, nay, of all time. "Literature," says Thomas A. Edison, "is a very good thing." And humor, if I may be allowed to paraphrase the "Wizard's" sage observation, is also a very good thing. It lightens the rough pathways. I cannot dedicate, I cannot consecrate, I cannot hallow this great—and I use that word advisedly—leavener. It is a contagious thing, humor, like the father of the college student who met the college professor. "I am delighted to meet you," said he, shaking hands warmly with the old professor, from whom, I may say, years of grubbing among books had not eliminated a keen sense of humor. "My son took algebra from you last year, you know." "Pardon me," said the professor, with a merry twinkle in his eye, "he was exposed to it, but he did not take it."

I am having a good deal of trouble, in my stuttering way, getting to my subject. And speaking of stuttering, it seems that one day in the Police Court the Judge asked the prisoner his name. "F-f-f-f!" said the prisoner, swallowing the atmosphere, and starting again. "F-f-f-f-f!" Swallowing still more atmosphere, he started again, "F-f-f-f-f!" "Officer! Officer!" exclaimed the Judge. "What is this man charged with?" "Begorra, Your Honor," said the officer, who was a son of the "Ould Sod," "an' I think he be charged with sody wather."

Well, readers, I think I am not overstating things very much this morning when I say that I never have enjoyed a book more than the little tome that is the subject of my little talk. In fact, so enthralled was I by it that I arrived here a little late. "Well, Mr. Adams," said Mr. Lambert to me, "You are a little late." "Yes," said I. "But better late than never."

The book that I refer to is called "Sparks of Laughter No. 2." When I picked it up, to while away what I often call an "idle hour," I had no notion that it would so greatly influence me. Yesterday if anybody had told me that ever, even after years of application, I could learn the forensic art, I should have called that man—and I hope the ladies will forgive me for a little plain speech—a prevaricator. After reading the book, especially the part called "Suggestions to Toastmasters" and "How to Tell a Funny Story," I feel that there is no audience I could not address with what our French brothers call *savoir faire*. "Toastmastering," the first piece of advice concludes, "is an ornamental art.

I have tried to show you some of its first principles. Use them and you will not go far wrong."

So much for that. It was the chapter on "How to Tell a Funny Story" that made the deepest impression on me, an impression as deep as the political orator, who was somewhat given to exaggerating, made on Martin W. Littleton, the well-known New York lawyer. "This fellow," said Mr. Littleton, "was addressing a meeting one night in my former home town, Dallas, Texas. He complained bitterly in his address of a certain alleged abuse of power.

"'Are we to take this lying down?' he roared. 'No, old chap,' called a little man from a back seat, 'the reporters 'll do that.'"

Let me read you from this chapter "How to Tell a Funny Story." "Memorize your stories. Get them down letter-perfect. Don't spoil your chance to earn a laugh by hesitating, stumbling, recalling, apologizing. Let the story come trippingly on the tongue. Face yourself in the mirror. Tell your stories to the man in the mirror. Satisfy him—completely—and then you may confidently expect to satisfy a larger audience."

Right here, dear readers, I want to say that I did that all last evening. I told stories, gazing at myself in the mirror, all yesterday afternoon. And my wife, who is my severest critic, hearing the gales of merriment issuing from my room, called to me and said, "You must be having a good time in there."

"I am," was my response. And, ladies and gentlemen, I *was*. And what is more, my friends, it was good, clean fun.

"Suppose you are at a banquet table and are called upon without warning to speak on a subject of which you know little," Mr. Anderson continues. "Self-deprecation would be appropriate, and if you did indeed speak to the purpose, so much greater your credit with your audience because you began so modestly. For example: 'Mr. Toastmaster and gentlemen, I am only so slightly familiar with the subject under discussion that I fear anything I might say would remind you of the man who recently was a Police Court prisoner.'—and then the Police Court stuttering story. Or: 'Mr. Toastmaster and gentlemen, I am obliged to plead dark ignorance of the subject that has been so ably analyzed and illumined, and if I should attempt to add to what has been said I should certainly fail to set up an intelligent contact with this audience, as did the young lady who for the first time in her life was seated, at a dinner, next to so high a dignitary as a Bishop,' and go on with the Bishop-pyjama story."

But, dear readers, the hour is growing late and there are other and brighter men on this great paper—yes, there are. I am afraid you are trying to flatter me—who may have something to say to you. In conclusion, I am going to read you Mr. Anderson's sound advice, which, if you follow, it will not be long until you hear, as Mr. Anderson says, "George, tell us the story you told the other day at the club." But above all, says Mr. Anderson, a few minutes a day, and every day, in mirror exercise. "The power," he concludes, "to tell a story is profitable. I have told you how to acquire this power—but whether or not dollars and power and satisfaction shall result depends altogether upon *yourself*."

And now, dear readers, I will leave you, somewhat like the colored man who, gazing at the final half-inch of a cheap cigar he was smoking, said, "Vell, Ay Tank Oi am g-g-g-gettin' to de end of mah rope."

* * *

At the savings bank hangs a picture of a bread line and a line at the teller's window. "On which line will you be at

60?" it asks. The likelihood is that we shall be at the teller's window, withdrawing enough to pay an income-tax instalment. And it is a more depressing thought than the speculation upon being in the bread line at 60.

Those who at 60 still are concerned with savings-bank deposits, are, it seems to us, the cautious and the fearful. Life has beaten the breadliners; but the savings-bank liners probably never even qualified to enter the fight.

* * *

SLEEP, PATIENT, SLEEP

A few soporifics culled from the remarks of physicians, surgeons, dentists, etc.

"There's a lot of it around just now."

* * *

"And first of all, don't worry, and get plenty of sleep."

* * *

"Well, well, and how is our patient this morning?"

* * *

"Pardon me, but who did your dentistry previously?"

"You have the constitution of a $\genfrac{}{}{0pt}{}{(man)}{(woman)}$ fifteen years younger—"

* * *

"If they were all like you, I guess we doctors would starve to death."

* * *

"Why, in a few weeks you'll probably be better than ever."

* * *

"Now, I won't hurt you."

* * *

"This may hurt you a *little*."

* * *

"Why don't you just go away for a few weeks?"

* * *

(*The next series of paragraphs appeared in The Conning Tower 1923–1927*)

The questionnaire thing is too much in the public mind. At a concert the other night, when a singer began "Who Is Sylvia?" a young woman said to the person next her, "June 17, 1775, known as the Ming Dynasty of Anne Boleyn, was written by Louisa M. Alcott."

* * *

We know too little about life to quarrel or to agree with Professor William Bradley Otis of the College of the City of New York, who made suggestions the other day to students contemplating suicide. He told them not to be too introspective, not to shrivel up in the face of the infinitude of physical matter; to avoid hurry; and to avoid cynics in life and literature. But at the close of the lecture Professor Otis read Bryant's "Thanatopsis," Henley's "Invictus," and Kipling's "If." It seems to us that poems like those are the ones you always find in the pocketbooks or scrapbooks of attempted or actual suicides. The chances are that an impressionable person, one who is afraid of life, who wishes to escape from its reality, will read "I am the master of my fate; I am the captain of my soul," and say to himself, "I am neither, and there is no hope that I ever shall be either." "If you can this and that," says Kipling, "you'll be a man, my son." The youth who feels inferior reads it, says to himself that he is none of these courageous things, therefore is not a man, and decides to end everything.

It strikes us that part of "Invictus" might be revised for the benefit of depressed youth:

In the fell clutch of circumstance,
     I've winced a lot and cried aloud;
Under the bludgeonings of chance,
     My head has frequently been bowed.

It matters not how dull the earth,
     How gray the sky that clouds above it,
The world is full of life and mirth,
     And even if it ain't, what of it?

* * *

Speaking of stars, there were many spangled nights recently. Low in the heavens one star was unusually luminous. It was visible through the trees that skirt Wide Waters Farm, which is near West Niles, which isn't far from Auburn, New York. Somebody asked Mr. Samuel Hopkins Adams, the farm's owner, what star it was. "Hell," said Mr. Adams, with that geniality that has earned him the sobriquet of "Honey" Adams, "people seem to think that I ought to know the name of every damned star they can see from my place, just because I've lived here so long."

The next night, as luck would have it, a visitor from New York—to whom the sight of any star probably was unwonted—asked his host what star that was, over there through the trees. "I don't know," said Mr. Adams, "I'm a stranger here myself."

* * *

AFTER READING HUNDREDS OF CRITICISMS OF BOOKS OF NON-PONDEROUS VERSE

"Delightful comic verse," they find,
And say, "It's perfect of its kind."
And yet, despite the critics' snort,
I'd give a lot to write that sort.

"Though vivid is the verse, and bright
As anybody now can write,
These tricky lines are easily done."
. . . I'd sell my soul to think of *one*.

* * *

"Remember," Mr. Otto H. Kahn once told the *Daily
Princetonian*, in an exclusive interview, "you can't lift
yourself by downing others." How did Mr. Kahn think
students get to be members of the Princetonian's board of
editors? They get there by downing others; editorial positions
on college publications are attained through competition.

It would be difficult to get the truth from almshouse
inhabitants as to their reasons for failure. The failure is even
more likely to lie about himself than is the success. But if
you could get the truth, many of the almshouse inmates
would say, we think, that they are poor because they believed seriously that they could advance without downing
others. . . . We do not believe, with the sport page poets,
that Life is Like a Football Game; but even those bards do
not parade the philosophy that life is like a tie game.

Why, the *Daily Princetonian* itself got ahead by downing
somebody. It is conceivable that the *Yale News* and the
Harvard Crimson both were attempting to get an interview
with Mr. Kahn, and that, in competition with the *Princetonian*, they failed.

It was well enough for Mr. Otto Kahn to tell the Prince-
ton boys—and others—to use their imagination, but the
advice is not utilitarian. The use of the imagination keeps
you at work unnecessarily long hours. You begin writing a
paragraph, and you imagine how pleasant and delightful it
would be doing something else, such as giving advice to the
Princetonian or riding on a giant liner bound for anywhere
at all. And, having imagination, it takes you an hour to
write a paragraph that, if you were unimaginative, would

take you only a minute. Or you might not write the paragraph at all.

Further deliberation on Mr. Otto Kahn's "Use your imagination" advice leads to the highly imaginative notion that imaginations should be treated like motor cars. Some of us would like to put our imaginations on sale in the Used Department; and some of us whose imaginations are eating their fool heads off are growing tired of paying storage charges.

There are also some of us who use our imaginations in speculating what we would do if we had as much wealth as Mr. Kahn possessed. We know what we imagine we'd do, for one thing; we'd throw our hat, reckless of its cost, into the air to demonstrate our joy at not having to depend for livelihood on an imagination.

* * *

President Remsen B. Ogilby of Trinity College said that he was taught to play poker by his mother when he was a child, and that therefore the game had no sinister allurements for him when he grew up. We don't see it that way, nor do we admit the "sinister." Our interpretation is that young Ogilby played poker entirely for fun—that is, for no stakes—and that he therefore decided, rightly, that it was a no-good game. If we had a son who got any fun out of playing poker for fun, we'd tie a box of chips to his leg and throw him into the river.

* * *

A WEAKLING'S BALLADE, WITH A SPECIALLY MIXED METAPHOR REFRAIN, OF SERFDOM

I am a swerveless and solid fellow;
Rock of Gibraltar they say am I;
Single-tracker as was Othello;
Rare is the ether in which I fly;

Beautiful letters the goal I try
　　And try to reach in the writers' race.
But, though mine aim be true and high,
　　I'm wax in the hands of a pretty face.

Nothing about me is weakly yellow.
　　Look at my jaw, and you'll holler, "My!
There is a man who says not 'Hello!'
　　There is a man who says 'Good-by!'
There is a man who would rather die
　　Than show of weakness a tiny trace."
Yet I admit, with a happy sigh,
　　I'm wax in the hands of a pretty face.

Loud are the tones in which I bellow
　　Vows to do nothing but versify,
Yet I'm a piece of diluted jello
　　If so a beauty—or two—I spy.
Though I endeavor to scale the sky,
　　Soaring on poems of wit and grace,
Somebody always comes through the rye—
　　I'm wax in the hands of a pretty face.

L'ENVOI

Honey, I'm honest; I never lie:
　　Safe in my heart is your certain place;
Safe, my darling, and you know why—
　　I'm wax in the hands of a pretty face.

* * *

(*The next series of paragraphs appeared in The Conning Tower 1934–1935*)

Again the professional writer is on the not uncelebrated spot. He buys a dollar shirt and it costs him $1.02. A publisher buys a story that he writes; that is, he sells a story, for

$100. But he doesn't get $102 for it. He gets $100, and part of that goes to the government in income tax.

A merchant buys $100,000 worth of stuff and finds that he has to sell it for $25,000. He deducts $75,000 for business losses. A poet spends $3,000 in attempting to gain a girl's affection, with no success. He writes a quatrain about the futility of love. May he deduct $2,999?

* * *

To the treasured Times Mr. Jean Brieux writes concerning the alleged recrudescence of smokers in subway cars. "There is nothing more objectionable," he says, "than the smell of cheap cigars kept burning and sometimes even kept smoking without shame or consideration." In his objection to subway smokers we are in utter harmony with Mr. Brieux. But it is doubted hereby that he is a cigar smoker. For the odor of a cheap cigar that has been allowed to expire is more noisome than that of one in operation. And to most objectors to cigars, whether they are smokers or not, the cost of a cigar has nothing to do with it. Your objector complains as much about a 75-cent cigar as he does about one that costs four cents. . . . Got a match, Mr. B.?

* * *

To the Collector of Internal Revenue: Is deductible the price of two cigars in 1933 as a present to a compositor, given in an effort to curry favor with same?

And how about the fortune that one spends "entertaining" a wife and family, in order to attain the sweet serenity so essential to the writing of satire?

And how about the quest for information? How about the $67 it cost us in the summer of 1933 to ascertain whether Russel Crouse was bluffing when he drew no cards? P. S. He wasn't.

* * *

The Metropolitan Life's actuarial department says that the average of expectation has increased; and that the old man of the eighties is now middle-aged. We refuse to be fooled. Years ago we discovered the exact point, the dead center of middle age. It occurs when you are too young to take up golf and too old to rush up to the net.

* * *

Every morning that timid reader, Mr. Caspar Milque-toast, discovers that a little more of his income has been shot from under him by the patriotic necessity of paying just one more tax. "Count that day won," he sings, "when, turning on its axis, this earth imposes no additional taxes."

* * *

Imminent is an impost on maple sugar and syrup. Which provokes:

> Government, spare that tree;
> Thy tax shall harm it not!

* * *

Absorption in work or play contributes to the illusion that the grave is not life's goal. Few of us are able to look back upon what we have done as an achievement, or as a contribution to the betterment of anybody's life. Yet while the work or play is on, it is a lot of fun if while you are doing one you don't constantly feel that you ought to be doing the other. One recalls what Whistler said to a student, who was smoking: "You should be very careful. You might get interested in your work and let your pipe go out."

* * *

VALENTINE

The ink is red,
The rent is due,

My hope is dead,
And how are you?

* * *

This is a broad country, geographically. It is the sort of country that exhorts men of education and training and incorruptibility to go into politics. When such men hold office or are appointed to office, they are called highbrows and brain trusters.

* * *

Whether Stuart Chase, the veteran overhead smasher of Redding, is the originator of the New Deal we are uncertain. His book "A New Deal," was announced before the Rooseveltian use of the phrase. And the coiner of Brain Trust was, according to Mr. Ernest K. Lindley's "The Roosevelt Revolution," Old Jim Kieran of the New York Times.

* * *

Mr. Stuart Chase was not the originator of the phrase, the New Deal, though it may have been through his book that the President popularized it. But in 1893, exhumes W. L. Werner, William Dean Howells published a one-act farce, "The Unexpected Guests," in which one of the characters says, "But now I've got to see that there's enough to eat, under this new deal."

How about the Brain Trust in the Civil War? General Sherman was the first superintendent of Louisiana Military Academy, where he taught Mathematics and English. General Robert E. Lee became president of what is now Washington and Lee University.

* * *

These things get into the language, and their originators seldom get even a corona of withered bays. Many persons still say "Say it ain't true, Joe." That was credited to a nameless small boy in Chicago, who was supposed to say it to Joe Jackson of the White—later Black—Sox, when he was told that Jackson had accepted a bribe in the World Series with Cincinnati. It was credited by James K. Mc-Guinness, then A. P. correspondent in Chicago, later Sun Dialist in a New York evening newspaper, and now a Big Shot in Hollywood.

* * *

In the Quill Mr. Bruce Bliven discusses censorship and its effect upon the future of free speech. Freedom of speech, he thinks, is less restricted here than in many other lands. He speaks of three important censorships at work in the American press: Of the audience; through one's economic position; and self-censorship, which he considers the most effective, the work of the invisible censor who sits in the brain and tells us "what isn't going to be popular," "what will make trouble," "what our readers (or advertisers, or owners) won't like." In many years of freedom from any censorship but self-censorship, we have no idea what isn't going to be popular, what will make trouble or what our readers, or advertisers, or owner won't like. Nor do we know what is going to be popular—or we'd write it like a shot this minute—what won't make trouble, and what readers, or advertisers or our owner will like. And don't think that we don't care, either. We should like to make readers, advertisers, and owner feel that our every word was priceless, important, and bursting with influence. We got freedom and we know many others of God's journalistic chillun who got it. That we don't do more with that freedom is the fault of our own limitations of expression. Some of these are self-imposed, consciously or not. Self-censorship, which we believe is an asset, is often the fear of writing or printing something pointless, or downright no-good. Pointlessness and worthlessness are elastic words, and one man's pointlessness is another man's barbed satire.

* * *

Mr. Mark Sullivan made an address to the Rotary International Congress at Detroit and said, in effect, among other things, that when the Administration called itself liberal it was committing verbal larceny. Now, Mr. Sullivan is a worker in words, and he ought to know that what is liberal to one man's notion is conservative or anarchistic to another's. Mr. Sullivan appealed to his hearers not to be seduced by words, nor to be misled by those cunning in the art of words. Why not? We prefer to be led by the articulate, as opposed to the glib; by the word-users rather than by the persons who cannot express ideas. "Do your thinking in terms of things, not words." Well, Mark, old kid, old boy, tell us how to do that. We, for one, refuse to be seduced by your peroration. How do we do our thinking in things, not words? Does that mean that the Administration talks too much and does too little? . . . As to that, nobody is more weary of thinking in words than we are. We should like to do our thinking with a racquet and a bathing suit, and not even read words, let alone assembling same.

* * *

ON THE FLEETNESS OF TIME

"Tu ne quaesieris, scire nefas—quem mihi, quem tibi"—
Horace: Book I, Ode II.

> Leuconoë, no longer grope
> About that silly horoscope;
> To know the future, yours and mine,
> Is dead against the laws divine.
>
> Better it is for us to bear
> To-morrow, be it foul or fair.

Filter your wines, for that is wise.
Who cares when this or that one dies?

Why, even as we converse to-day,
The jealous present slips away.
How futile mortal plot and plan!
Come, seize the present while you can!

* * *

The Lancashire mills won't export any more cotton yarn to Germany, because, they say, Germany won't pay. Does Germany pay the non-German munition makers that sell to her? Our guess is yes. A nation ostensibly without money always seems to have money enough to buy arms. Such a nation reminds us of an impecunious drunkard who never has car fare, but always has money or credit to buy liquor.

* * *

Reading of many novels convinces us that the best part of the fiction therein is the notice to the effect that the characters are all purely imaginary.

* * *

Perhaps everybody has his ambition for one thing that will benefit humanity. Ours is a bonfire in the Grand Canyon of all the paper towels in the world.

* * *

One of the questions asked in the Home Owners' Manual, issued by the Federal Housing Administration, is "Can you find things in closets?" Yes, boys. In the closet designated for our apparel we can find 1 pr. women's tennis shoes, 2 1932 evening gowns, 1 sport dress, 4 prs. boys' knickers, and 1 Mickey Mouse bathing suit.

* * *

Mr. H. G. Wells's "Experiment in Autobiography" is, to our notion, a deep and engrossingly exciting book. It seems so to us because of our conviction that Wells's fiction had a profound effect on the thought and actions of his generation. This book is written with the same bright liveliness that is as much a part of him as his fingernails. Some of it is as detached as if he were writing about somebody else, just as in most of his fiction he is writing about himself. The book has another common factor with fiction. Wells's life is in the Cinderella pattern. And in his life story, the most interesting part—to us—is his childhood and his early start; the time before Cinderella arrives at the ball. Cinderella's dance program is the least interesting of her records.

What Wells thought and felt while he was writing those books that we have read—all his fiction from "The Wheels of Chance" to "Mr. Bulpington of Blup"—is fascinating stuff to read. Years ago, in the "Love and Mr. Lewisham" and "Kipps" days, we naïvely wondered how Wells could know so much of our inner thoughts when we never had confided in him. We didn't know that we were laying a wreath on his head, the kind that all writers covet. It must be sweet music, no matter how often a writer hears it—and Wells must have heard it often—to hear "How could you know all that?"

* * *

Some insomniacs take this or that potion. Our favorite soporific is the announcement by some official that this or that department will be run with no consideration of politics.

* * *

On mornings after election children generally want to know whether their admirable sire won't please be president or governor or mayor next election. The parent's answer may be to the effect that the holding of such a high office necessitates much and continued absence from home and that governors and such have little or no time to devote to their offspring. "Hey," was one comment yesterday, "you better keep on being a papa."

* * *

FROM THE NEW ENGLAND PRIMER

In *Autumn* (Fall)
They kick the ball

Replete with sleep
From *Bed* I leap.

In *Chicago* Ill.,
They used to kill.

David, defiant,
Slew a giant.

The *Emu* bird
Is a cross-word.

In Flushing there
Once was a *Fair*.

The proffered *Glass*
I never pass.

My books and *Heart*
Are far apart.

Many an *Ignoramus*
Has become famous.

Job was poor-
Er than you're.

Some people pan
The *Ku Klux Klan*.

Like Washington, I
Do loathe a *Lie*.

B. *Mussolini*
Adores zucchini.

On Ararat
Old *Noah* sat.

I loathe *Obadiah*,
Who says "Toots, h'yah!"

Once E. A. *Poe*
Drank H_2O.

The good *Queen* Bess ex-
Ecuted Essex.

No bed of *Roses*
Hath Robert Moses.

Sticks and *Stones*
For Germany's Kohns.

Too much *Truth*
Is uncouth.

Slimy and deep
Was *Uriah* Heep.

On stage and screen
The famous Queen

Known as *Victoria*
Never would boria.

H. G. *Wells*
Everything tells.

Xerxes, once chief,
Is on relief.

Youth and Age
Are far from sage.

Young *Zaccheus*, he
Cussed Franklin D.
And all D. C.

* * *

WOMEN CAN'T PLAY POKER

The hour is growing late, and there are many other speakers, though none better. Your toastmaster has asked me to speak on "Women Can't Play Poker." As a former Paying Teller of the Thanatopsis Literary and Inside Straight Club, I know whereof I whereas.

The first game of the T. L. and I. S. Club was played at the apartment then jointly occupied by two recently returned members of the 1918 *Stars and Stripes* staff, Pvt. Harold W. Ross, now editor of the *New Yorker;* and Pvt. (now Col.) John T. Winterich. Sgt. Alexander Woollcott, Heywood Broun, and I were in that first game. I gave it the name, which I stole from Sinclair Lewis' *Main Street*. In time there were added John Peter Toohey, George S. Kaufman, and Robert E. Sherwood. Now and then others played here and there; but never women. Well, hardly ever. I mention no names, partly because I am no cad who bandies a woman's name about in a place like this, and partly because, except for Neysa McMein, Mrs. Herbert Bayard Swope, and my wife, I forget who they were. There is a common error that I am about to correct. It often is assumed that men feel freer, especially orally, when women aren't around. This may have been true Before My Time, when men were supposed to linger at table with the port and brandy while the ladies went upstairs to get away from the naughty stories that were supposed to be concomitants of cigars and cigarettes. But it is not true of the games I have played in, averaging once a week for twenty-five years. There is little talk that goes on in our games that isn't for women's pretty ears. Why, we often have women kibitzers, and the talk is just the same when they are there as when they leave.

But in our games everybody, which includes men playing in the game for the first time, knows the value of the chips. Everybody knows the limit, the sequence of betting, as well as the number of cards each player draws. Which is what women *don't* do. Women—save your stationery, girls; I know you are exceptions. It's what you all say. You *love* to play. I know very well that you *love* to play.

But women hold up the game to ask repeatedly how much the blue chips are worth, and the red, and the white; how much they are allowed to bet; they have to be reminded that they're shy, that it's their turn to deal, to bet, to shuffle—all the things that in a men's game go without saying.

We play poker, which is to say poker—one round of stud and three rounds of draw. Five cards. But Virgil, probably a dice player in a men's game, said *varium et mutabile semper femina*. Which translated means, "Women always want to play variations"—seven-card high-low stud, one-eyed jacks wild, spit in the ocean, baseball, dealer's choice.

It may be said that we who won't allow women to play in our game don't know: that we just won't let them play, and how do we know that we don't want them to? Well, I'm glad that question came up. We have had women play in our game, and others than those whom I have mentioned. If they were women whose husbands were in the game, the husbands would have to pay the losses, and of course get none of the winnings. Also, women have peculiar notions about quitting. A woman is ahead $22. "Come on, dear," she says, "you've got to get up early tomorrow." Dear is $218 to the bad and has Loser's Insomnia, as opposed to a common disease known as Winner's Sleeping Sickness. But he is in what is known in our game as Hell's Hole, Alabama; he doesn't want to quit. For the belief persists that if he plays another hour, or three, he may get even, or even win. But the chances are that Dear quits, losing $218. Now, suppose he wins $218, and she loses $22. Therefore he loses $196.

That, of course, is just money. But we play for money, and our motto is the opposite of Grantland Rice's famous poem about the Great Official Scorer. For with us, it doesn't matter how you play the game, but whether you win or lose.

Oh, yes. Another thing that women do is to tell stories, or at least talk, during their deal, holding a card poised until they finish the story. And the chances they take! In the old days, when women were allowed in some games, my wife, whose name is Esther, would have, say, a ten and a seven of hearts, and draw three cards. Two cards of one suit, so nicknamed by the late Alexander Woollcott, were known to the Thanatopsis Club as an Esther flush.

And women brood over their hands. If her hand wins, she should have bet more. She weeps. If it loses, she shouldn't have been in at all; she shouldn't have called. She weeps.

Women, however, tell the truth. When they play poker they are honest. They won, they lost, and how much. Men lie. Men always either win or Come Out Even. If, as happens in most poker games, somebody loses, he goes home and says that he lost about one-tenth of what he lost. Or he wins, and he often chops that in half for home consumption. Also he lies about the time the game broke up, or at least when he quit. Men do this for two reasons. A man says that he won or lost X dollars. Well, if he can afford to win or lose X dollars, not to say wasting that time, he can certainly afford to buy this or that, or to take her to a costly night club and stay there until 3 A.M. Didn't he play poker last night until 7 A.M.? Didn't he win $72? Didn't he lose $72? If he won $72, why can't he spend it? If he lost $72, why can't he spend another $72 on an evening with Her?

It often has occurred to me, in the many times that I've seen *Life with Father*, that if Father Day had played poker, he'd have had a good argument about it, much sounder than that economic principle of Vinnie's, when she got that pug dog for nothing. Incidentally, Mr. Howard Lindsay and Mr. Percy Waram, both of whom have been Father Day hundreds of times, play in our weekly game.

Nowadays thousands of women are working. They are not the poker-playing kind. And neither are the poker-playing kind. For poker is adventure, a man's game; adventure is a masculine passion. Non-playing, or Security, is a feminine passion. And a right good passion, too.

Of course, the true reason men don't like to play poker with women is that we are resentful. We are jealous that they so often beat us at our own games that we keep them out of poker, our little game.

And women are realists, which we poker players are not. When I play, I immerse myself in the game; it's an escape, it's fairy-tale stuff. It's the idiot's mirage; the phony notion that you get something for nothing. It is a holdover from playing marbles for keeps.

Girls, you can't—that is, you may not—play in our

Monday-night game. And in my logical mind, in my reason, I know that you are missing nothing; even that I—and my many Little Ones—would be better off not to play. The rest of me feels that you don't know how much fun we have, and how much relaxation, and how— Okay, Crouse. Just about finished. I'll be there in ten minutes.

* * *

IMPERATIVE MOOD

(With a Bow to Gilbert's "To the Terrestrial Globe")

Blow, blow, thou winter wind,
 Whirling the sleets and snows!
Blow, keeping me not in mind.
 (It blows.)

Weep an thou wilt, my fair,
 Though sorrow on me creeps.
Let not thy girl-heart care!
 (She weeps.)

Give me more love or more
 Disdain; on doubt none lives.
Give either, I implore!
 (She gives.)

Shine on, oh harvest moon!
 (You know the well-known lines;
You know the hackneyed tune.)
 (It shines.)

* * *

Students and professors of journalism should study the differences between the ethics, or, at any rate the common practices, of forty years ago and those of today. Recently

Mrs. LaGuardia bought $371.09 worth of furniture at the store of W. and J. Sloane. All the papers said so. Forty years ago they would have said that she made a purchase at a Fifth Avenue shop; this silly practice was indulged in in the superstitious fear that such mention would offend other advertisers. In 1903, Mr. William K. McKay, managing editor of the Chicago Journal, advised us, a pale young columnist, in part as follows: "Write whatever you please, but don't use any unprintable words. Many of our advertisers are sensitive, and will think that you mean them."

* * *

AMERICA, THE BEAUTIFUL

The women have their hair waves,
   And fret about their girth;
And comics on the air waves
   Indulge in song and mirth.

On links too many to number
   The weekend golfers play,
And some may drink, or slumber
   The bombless night away.

And some may toil and worry,
   If but so be their bent,
And some nor speed nor hurry
   In competent content.

And some seek liberation
   From pleasure and from ease,
And how I love the nation
   Where I write rhymes like these!

* * *

It seems that there was a poker game at Warm Springs, Ga., in which Mr. Harry Hopkins was supposed to have won a Tidy Sum. Mr. Ralph Smith, who runs a column in the Atlanta Journal, says that it was a five-handed game, and that the other players were Secretaries Morgenthau and Ickes, Mr. Rexford Tugwell, and Mr. Marvin McIntyre. Mr. Hopkins won $1.38. We are off the lot of them, and we sigh for the good old Harding days, when poker players were men. Playing poker for stakes in which a big winning is $1.38 is no fun; it is no fun unless you play for more than you can afford to win or lose. Rather than play in that Warm Springs game we'd rather read a book or see a play that we didn't like.

* * *

THE END OF CLEOPATRA

Then there was the Roman poet Horace, the good friend of F. P. A. . . . Horace said in one of his poems that it was a time for dancing *pulsanda tellus*, for striking the ground with flying feet.—New York Times.

Nunc est bibendum
pulsanda tellus . . .

—Horace: Book I, Ode 37.

Now is the time to drain the cup
That cheers, with shouts of "Bottoms up!"
To feast; to tap it as you go
Upon the light unfettered toe.

Hitherto it had been a crime
To touch that Cæcuban sublime
While still a wild and frenzied queen
Tried to disrupt the Roman scene.

That woman, with her rotten crew
Of crooks and lechers! crazy, too,

Enough to nurture any hope,
For she is drugged with Fortune's dope.

Vanished the smile from her proud lips
When Cæsar burned her pretty ships;
Altered her wine-deluded cheer
Into the rigorous fact of fear.

His galleys gave her ships a shove,
Even as the hawk pursues the dove,
Or as the hunter makes to flee
The hare o'er snowy Thessaly.

A noble queen, she showed no fear
For death upon the pointed spear;
And scorned to flee, forevermore
To dwell upon some hidden shore.

And gazed she with unruffled brow
Upon her castle, fallen now;
Bravely the asp she nursed, that she
Might grace no glorious victory.

* * *

"Poor Della," wrote Harry Hansen in yesterday's W.-T.,
speaking of John Held's "I'm the Happiest Girl in the
World." "She gets married, and that, I take it, is an end
to her public life. She had lovely legs, but who wants to see
lovely legs at the breakfast table?" Quiet, please, gentlemen;
you deafen us.

Perhaps Mr. Hansen would like to read "A Husband's
Garden of Verses," of which the following, with a little luck,
may be one:

A wife should always say what's true,
And speak when she is spoken to,
And have lovely legs at the breakfast table.
At least, as far as she is able.

Why, Mr. Hansen, how it was in Davenport, Iowa, we don't know; but in Illinois they used to say, "Yes, sir, a cup o' coffee and a pair of lovely legs; that's my breakfast, day in and day out. Yes, sir."

Maybe Mr. Hansen prefers a couple of lovely eggs.

So many comments have been received upon Harry Hansen's rhetorical question about the sub-tabular matutinal legs that there is nothing to do but for Omar to smite 'is bloomin' lyre:

A pair of legs beneath the Breakfast Table;
A pot of coffee, strong and colored sable
Beside me singing in the Percolator—
Greater than Grable Thou, and I than Gable!

* * *

PERCY HAMMOND

1873-1936

Percy Hammond died on Saturday at midnight. The public that has been reading him for thirty years will feel the loss; his friends among the critics will feel it; the men who worked with him on the Herald Tribune, who had grown deeply attached to him in his fifteen years in New York, feel it with ineffable acuteness. And some of us whose friendship with Percy began thirty-five years ago, whose manner of life and expression had such a strong influence that it became a part of ours, find words now an immovable mass of blurred syllables.

Percy Hammond was, to our notion, the most glamorous of Chicago newspaper men in 1901. At that time he was covering the City Hall for the City Press, which corresponds to our New York City News Association; also he was press agent for the Grand Opera House, owned by the Hamlins, whose fortune had been gleaned from the wide sale of Hamlin's Wizard Oil, an emollient that gentlemen in the county fair and medicine show professions vaunted as a panacea. He was known, as we have said from time to time, as the Paid Piper of Hamlin. It is possible that George Wharton, one of Chicago's wittiest phrasemakers, gave him this nickname; it is more likely that Percy gave it to himself.

That was the year when "The Wizard of Oz" opened at the Grand Opera House. Night after night Percy's friends— Walter Whiffen, Sam Gerson, Bill Moore, and even Burns Mantle, at that time the Inter Ocean's drama critic, would occupy a box. And two years later, when "Babes in Toyland" played during the summer and autumn of 1903, the group of dramophiles was augmented by Clifford Raymond, Richard Henry Little, Arthur Sears Henning, and now and then William Hard. Nightly attendance was almost compulsory. Percy, still a Cadiz, Ohio, boy at heart, mingled not with the stars, who were William Norris, Bessie Wynn, Mabel Barrison, and Amy Ricard. Percy introduced us all to the lovely choristers, Mobel Frenyear, Jean Carnegie, Lesbia Grealis, Virginia Foltz, Helen Hahn, Bertha Krieghoff—and we are confident that a week ago Percy could have recalled a few more, also without benefit of reference. There were many night suppers, necessarily frugal, at the Bismarck, the Edelweiss, and Vogelsang's. It was about the time when Richard Carle, in "The Tenderfoot," was singing "I met my love in the Alamo, when the moon was on the rise." So the Grand Opera House stage door anthem became "I met my love in the alleyway, when the 'Babes' were at the Grand."

Percy Hammond, the only journalist in that semi-rural Chicago carrying a cane, became a reporter on the Chicago

Evening Post. In 1909, when Bert Leston Taylor was an editor of Puck, he got a letter from Mr. Joseph Medill Patterson, asking who was the best critic in New York for the Chicago Tribune to acquire. Taylor wrote to say that Percy Hammond of the Chicago Evening Post was better than anybody in New York.

He became the Chicago Tribune's critic of the drama, from which fortress he frequently kidded the trousers off what seemed to him the more spurious and pretentious of the errant mimes. It was at this time that Mrs. Robert Mantell, wife of a well known Shakespearean actor, gazed at the no-longer-slender Hammond, saying, "Ah, that one so gross should write of Art!"

Hammond's decision to come to New York was made a week or two after the death, in 1921, of Bert Leston Taylor, who had been the Chicago Tribune's columnist. The Tribune ordered Hammond to succeed Taylor; he spent three or four days writing one—his first and only—column; said that he couldn't do it. We had been trying to get Hammond to come to the New York Tribune since 1914. His 1914 letter said: "The town grows more hopeless daily, and I have become ambitious for the first time in my life to venture into New York."

So in 1921, on a visit to Chicago, we tried again. He gave Mr. Patterson an ultimatum, and wrote "I am now in the ominous umbra of his displeasure." . . . And in the same letter, when "Dulcy" was playing Chicago, he wrote: "I met Miss Fontanne at Joe Ryerson's the other night and she said she was hurt because you did not call on her Sunday evening. But she was pleased with the report that I gave her of your comment on her beauty and that of her performance."

Well, the New York Tribune sent its managing editor, Mr. W. O. McGeehan, out to Chicago to sign Percy up. And he wrote: "I'll be happier in New York than I am here under the circumstances, provided that I can get away with it. I like McGeehan, who impressed me as a regular human being; and I take it from you and him and Julian Mason among others that Mr. Reid is aces. Burns Mantle writes that after a year of misery in New York I'll have it as much my own way in New York as I have it now in Chicago. Which cheers but does not inebriate me. Tremble, Stephen Rathbun!"

For longer than the first year New York frightened Hammond; and nameless persons, later to become his staunchest praisers, would meet us and say, "Where did you get the idea that this fellow could write?"

He wrote of the fears of a reviewer nearing "the fertile gardens and billowy fields of Broadway. The scores of actors who have said, 'Broadway needs you, my boy!' now put the dread lump of terror in his throat with sad owl songs, portentous of disaster. . . . Fellow journalists warn him that the readers of New York dramatic reviews are smart and urbane, the deep purple of the playgoers, and that he must amend the gauche practices indigenous to prairie criticism. He will miss the paternal compassion with which the Chicago Tribune, the great wounded journal he had abandoned, forgave his frequent infractions of its dignity and reticence." And lest any thought his mood antic, "let me say," he wrote, "that it is but a whistling to keep from being afraid. Gone are the brave dreams picturing Broadway as a chafed lion, cowering beneath my haughty huntsman's gaze; and in their place some visions of an affrighted mongrel pursuing a fleet but reluctant course down the Rialto."

To write about Percy Hammond thus, instead of with the dignity that thanatopsis is supposed to inspire, may also be a whistling to keep from being afraid, afraid of a world without Percy Hammond.

* * *

THE LADY

There is a garden in her face;
　　She walks in beauty like the night
No maid in all of Samothrace
　　Is half so fine a sight.

Upon her lovely countenance
　　She puts in but two hours a day;
Upon apparel's elegance
　　But three hours flit away.

At music's shrine she fails to kneel,
　　Nor worships she the bards sublime.
She says—and wide is her appeal—:
　　"I simply don't get time."

* * *

*(The next series of paragraphs appeared in The Conning
Tower 1936–1937)*

It seems to us that those who scream the loudest about
the Freedom of the Press want all the privileges of freedom
with none of its responsibilities. The trouble with the problem is that the yellower the press, the more plausible it makes
its appeal to a public. The conservative public, or the otherwise intelligent public, is an ostrich; it dismisses the whole
matter by saying, "I never read that paper," or "I wouldn't
have the paper in the house."

And yet we would not have a single shackle on the press's
freedom. The law of libel is enough. You may say that taste
is another brake, but one editor's taste is another editor's
outrageous obscenity, which may be called by him—possibly
sincerely—red-blooded courage.

* * *

When the man you like switches from what he said a year ago, or four years ago, he is a broadminded person who has courage enough to change his mind with changing conditions. When a man you don't like does it, he is a liar who has broken his promises.

And Republicans and Democrats on February 12 quote the Gettysburg Address, to prove that Lincoln would have been on their side.

* * *

Indignation is felt in England because Maxim Litvinoff, the Soviet Foreign Commissioner, said of King Edward that he was "a mediocre young Englishman, who reads no more than one newspaper a day." That probably would be the London Times, though it might be—we hope that it is—the Manchester Guardian. But mediocrity in a ruler is something that endears him to the people, to whom mediocrity would be a promotion. And as for reading one newspaper a day, most of us don't do even that. We read a good many headlines, and one or two other things, in one newspaper a day.

We are not certain that the more newspapers one reads, the more mediocre one becomes; or maybe the more one approaches mediocrity, the more newspapers one reads. We know how it is; we read all the papers every day. This habit has gone on so long that our mind has been a pulp, convinced of everything and credulous of nothing.

* * *

The average taxi driver, it seems to us, is like the average voter; conditions usually are wrong. Every weather prospect displeases, and only the non-passenger is vile. "How is hacking?" you ask. "Terrible," he says. "It's so cold that everybody stays at home, or doesn't want to ride on these icy streets." And when things are fair and warmer, "It's such nice weather that people'd rather walk than ride in cabs."

But our favorite is the driver who said, "I can complain, but I don't, especially out loud. Don't do no good, and makes the passenger feel it's his fault."

* * *

BASEBALL NOTE

In winter, when it's cold out,
Appears the baseball holdout;
In spring, when it is warm out,
He gets his uniform out.

* * *

The trouble with this country is that there are too many politicians who believe, with a conviction based on experience, that you can fool all of the people all of the time.

* * *

Inflation has its benefits. We know somebody we wouldn't touch with a twenty-foot pole.

* * *

What is the right age for what? "His," declares Commissioner Valentine, of Mr. Marcantonio, "is the arrogance and immaturity of youth." The Supreme Court is popularly known as Nine Old Men. There must be a day or two in a man's life when he is the precise age for something important.

* * *

"Work," says our favorite diarist, Mrs. Eleanor Roosevelt, "when you have no interruptions, when you can look out at the landscape and in at the open fire, does not seem like work." Well, we know different. We have looked out at the landscape and in at the open fire for hours at a time, and the first thing we knew five hours had elapsed and nothing like work had been done at all. In order to do work we set our eyes at the pulled-down curtain and turn our back to the open fire. Even then, dear diarist, the work is nothing more immortal than the stuff we do in the office.

* * *

"Indeed," said Miss Dorothy Thompson yesterday, writing of the floods, "the catastrophe is too soon forgotten. Were men's memories longer they would prepare against its recurrence." They would; and yet Noah, with his gopher-wood ark, was the only man in the Bible that prepared.

Men's memories are short. They don't prepare against the recurrence of war, and not much against the recurrence of the poverty that comes with wide unemployment. They don't remember the campaign promises of politicians; and the politicians don't remember them, either.

* * *

Our favorite diarist, Mrs. Eleanor Roosevelt, has qualified as a columnist, although her stuff is only about a third of a column. She has written about how hard it is to have to write a piece every day. "Really," she says, "it is not all beer and skittles when you are a seemingly carefree lady and still have something in the background which you must do." After a few more years of it, Mrs. R., you won't be seemingly carefree. You'll be obviously care-ridden; it will be with you, that millstone, all your waking hours, which gradually will increase. But don't write about the difficulty of writing; we do it too much; and our destructive critics tell us to desist from that old tune. Nobody cares.

* * *

Miss Fannie Hurst said that writing is a difficult task. She was taking issue with Miss Agnes Repplier, who said that it was "perilously easy" to write a book. Our guess is that Miss Repplier believes that writing is a difficult task, and that she meant that it is perilously easy to have a tenth-rate book published. Any book reviewer's desk is piled high with books received every morning. The successes, which is to say books that pay their way to author or even to publisher, are rare; the books which have distinction in writing are rarer. Writing, our opinion is, is a difficult task—good writing or bad writing. The only fun in the world, as the late Percy Hammond used to say so often that we are getting to believe that we said it, is not writing.

* * *

Mr. Milton Wright has written a book called "The Art of Conversation," and in it there are some snappy answers to some not too snappy questions. A good many of them seem like straw men to be bowled over, and they assume that the questioner is without resources. In the World office callers, generally on jury duty in the neighborhood, would drop in. One of these called on Deems Taylor in the cubbyhole contiguous to ours. "Well," said the caller, "how's music?" "Dandy," said Mr. Taylor. "How's boredom?"

* * *

In last Sunday's Times Book Review Mr. P. W. Wilson speaks of Caesar's Commentaries, "which, to this day, are read in schools and colleges." In a decreasing number of schools and colleges, it may be added. Chemistry and Physics are regarded as more important to graduates than Latin; the idea that a student is incapable of getting a little Latin with his Science is part of the college coddling system. There are times when the so-called higher education afflicts us with what used to be called the vapors.

* * *

Our sympathies always are with strikers. Usually they don't strike until long after their employers refuse to meet requests; none of them wants to strike and be out of work for even a day, let alone a number of weeks. And generally the appeal to the strikers by employers is to their "loyalty." Now, it seems to us that a worker should be loyal to his employer, and that an employer should be loyal to his workers. But the workers in whose confidence we have been tell us that they are supposed to furnish ninety per cent of the loyalty.

* * *

LOVE SONG

As I love my noisy neighbor,
  As Hitler loves the Jew,
As Capital loves Labor—
  That's how I love you.

As Puritan loves enjoyer,
  As Custer loved the Sioux,
As worker loves employer—
  That's how I love you.

* * *

Our favorite diarist tells her readers that she was glad that she didn't have to write a column, meaning about a third of a column, on Saturday, "for," Mrs. Roosevelt says, "from early morning until we got on the train that night, I scarcely had time to think." Mrs. Roosevelt is still in the kindergarten stage of columning. Veteran columnists know that thinking and columning do not always go hand in hand; as they know that there are times when the more they think, the less they write. And on lucid days they know that if they thought enough, they wouldn't write anything.

* * *

WHAT MAKES MY MOUTH WATER

As I was saying to my son only yesterday, *Forsan et haec olim meminisse iuvabit*—which means, It still makes my mouth water to think of McIntyre and Heath, the Georgia Minstrels, as their 1896 variety act was called. McIntyre, as Alexander, had been taken away from dat liv'y stable by the glib Heath, to be a minstrel; they were stranded on a railway siding; Alexander was urged on by Heath, or Henry, with stories about a biscuit bush and a ham tree; he was further tortured by a description of "roast beef and mashed potatoes, with the gravy—not comin' out—no sir, dat gravy was just oozin' out, Alexander." That picture had such an effect upon my youthful salivary glands that I could hardly wait until I got home for supper—I never grew to the sophisticated point of speaking naturally of dinner in the evening—and if we had roast beef and mashed potatoes that night, life was heaven. It makes my mouth water to think of sitting there in the Olympic Theater, Chicago, listening to the famished McIntyre. (Ten minutes elapse.) I go downstairs to rummage in the icebox or, as the moderns who use these horseless-carriage contraptions call it, the refrigerator. Cold roast beef and raw peas, both wonderful.

A highly susceptible trencherman am I. After McIntyre and Heath's roast beef, there was "The Belle of New York." Well do I recall a scene in Huyler's, and after the matinee I went over to Huyler's and got a ten-cent piece of Old Fashioned Molasses Candy, which the red curtain said was Fresh Every Hour.

Never have I seen a play in which the actors were at table that I didn't vicariously sit with them. There was "The First Year." And there were "Dinner at Eight" and "You Can't Take It with You." And those breakfasts in "Life with Father"! After that opening night in 1939 when

I first heard Mr. Day say, "Those kippers are *good!*" I had kippers the next morning for breakfast, and they were at least as good as the stage fish. And when Mr. Day complained about the coffee, I felt sorry for him, because it was a matter of years before I could convince a cook, although I paid her salary and I paid for the coffee, that I wanted one cup of coffee, and only one, and that one strong, using as much coffee as she would use for three cups of her idea of coffee.

Why, it made me hungry when Weber and Fields used to talk about breakfast, in the days when it was hokum humor to make fun of the uncooked cereal. "You eat dis shredded hay?" said Weber. "Sure," said Fields. "With plenty of sugar and cream, you could hardly notice it."

It is those who write about the glories of the table who make my mouth water; those whose literary boards groan beneath the weight of—to continue the rural press's description—many toothsome viands. I can't find that book of Favorite Recipes of Famous Authors, but I remember nothing except the ending of Montague Glass's bouilla-baisse—"God, but I'm hungry!" Many a dinner I had at Glass's, all of them good.

It isn't by chance that certain writers like to describe comestibles. Ferberiana, from "Dawn O'Hara" to the New Orleans markets and restaurants of "Saratoga Trunk, are full of goodies; Miss Ferber is just about the eatingest author there is. The autobiographical "A Peculiar Treasure" often tells what's cooking. "The soup was served in a tureen. The meat was carved at the table, the vegetables dished. I have that old soup tureen, a creamy china with a tawny oakleaf pattern. I never see it that my mouth doesn't water. The soup was almost always chicken soup with noodles (hand-rolled, homemade, hair-fine) or beef soup with marrow balls, a clear strong golden brew. When the cover was removed a fragrant steam arose . . . 'Here comes the soup! Look at this roast stuffed chicken, brown and crisp. I can see the slices melting away from the glittering carving knife.'" Why, her very titles are hunger compelling—"Roast Beef Medium" and "Come and Get It."

And today, if you get an invitation to lunch, dinner, or supper at Miss Ferber's, Upper Stepney, Connecticut, go, unless you prefer a drug store sandwich, which usually is made of bread discarded by the blotter manufacturers. You get amazingly good stuff at Ferber's, and plenty, so that if you want three helpings of duck, you have it. You may get a scornful glance from the ethereal guests, whose stare seems to echo a framed motto on the wall of a boardinghouse in the Ann Arbor of the nineties. It was "God Hates a Glutton," which, if true, automatically endowed all the boarders ($3.50 a week) with heavenly grace.

There are some joys that I don't get enough of: clams; lobster stew as I once had it at Jake Powers's where his folks lived near East Sebago, Maine; the fish chowder brewed on Sutton Island, Maine, by the late Rachel Field, which I apostrophized with—sorry, "The Melancholy Lute" is out of print:—

> Loud is my praise, or even louder,
> For Mrs. Arthur Pederson's chowder,
> It had such qualities and traits
> I had to have three brimming plates.

And that reminds me that I have gone on record many times about my loves and hatreds of the table. As for instance:—

> For steak that's rare
> I deeply care.

> I yell and whisper
> For bacon crisper.

To my trust I were false if I
Said I liked salsify.

And I must confess
That I don't like cress.

For starch of corn
I have but scorn.

An' boy, Ah sutton-
Ly likes mah mutton.

I always ask twice
For Spanish rice.

But I get sick
At sauces thick.

For goodness's sake,
Why marble cake?

But sauce caramel?
Mamma! that's swell!

Drinks with gin
I hate like sin;

But the lyre I strum
For drinks with rum.

For peanut butter
My hate is utter.

When we have cold lamb
I holler "Damn!"

Nor would I beg
For a hard-boiled egg.

Pudding of rice
Is not so nice;

But pie of plum—
Yum! Yum! Yum! Yum!

Perhaps if or when starvation perching at the horseman's
back will not be unseated, I shall be glad to have a drug
store sandwich and a cup of drug store brown-colored hot
water, with milk—only, however, if starving. How they
assemble these sandwiches I don't know; or why they think
that scalding heat is coffee's only requisite. Our cook, who
long since has known that I like one cup of strong coffee,—
and not three of weak,—sat next to me at a performance of
"Life with Father." When the elder Day asked how coffee
beans and water can achieve the brew in his breakfast cup,
Delia said, "Just like home, Mr. Adams." My son Anthony,
then fourteen, sat next to me at an earlier performance.
Towards the end of the play he finally said, after one of
Mr. Day's outbursts, "Pop, he's just like you. And he's
right, too."

There is a difference, of course, between liquids scalding
and liquids tepid. I hate soup that is so hot that you can't
taste it, or coffee so hot—the drug store formula—that you
can't taste it. Cf. the James Whitcomb Riley poem about
the coffee "my mother used to make," ending, "Yer coffee's
mighty hot." Women! They're all alike, or worse. From the
days when as a child I blew on the soup in my soupspoon,
and was reprimanded for same, to yesterday morning when
I almost missed the bus—and speaking of the old days, I
can still recall when I drove a car to the station for the 7:34

train because I was trying to cool the coffee so as to be able to drink it—from then to now, these women—relations and cooks—have one sentence that puts me in my place. It is:— "Food *should* be hot."

The soldiers of today have good cooks; and in World War I the army's cooks were good, too. But dozens of times, when I was billeted in some French town, and had to sit at the family table, the woman would always apologize for the paucity of the courses and the meagerness of the portions, not to say the quality. But always a wonderful soup, veal or beef so tender and so flavored that you can't get it at home like that, and about thirty-five dollars' worth of oil-drenched salad, not to say fruit and cheese. But apologies are the way of the cook. Alas! Where are those men and women at Neufchâteau and Meaux and Nancy and Boucq and Langres who told us that the Americans were saving France, little dreaming that it was being saved for enslavement.

I am no crank. We were taught to eat what was set before us; and we did, for it usually was excellent. I remember our Sunday breakfasts. One Sunday we had codfish balls—made of codfish, not of potatoes—and baked beans which had been put in the oven Saturday afternoon; and the next Sunday we had scraped beefsteak, with raw eggs on top. Those breakfasts alternated in our house for at least fifteen years. What we knew as Scraped Meat you may now get as Steak Tartare, which is garnished with a lot of lettuce, piccalilli, raw onion, anchovies, and what not. It's as hard to get it reft of these Persian pomps as it is to get a sandwich unencumbered by wilted lettuce and a fifth-rate pickle. And unless you or somebody who fears your scorn mixes the salad dressing it is too vinegary. It should be about 95 percent oil. Don't argue with me.

Remind me some time to tell you of the consternation, almost calling for a meeting of the board of directors, that it throws a restaurant into if you ask for an apple. Apple sauce, baked apple, apple cake, apple pie, yes. But you'd think the waiters had no knowledge of the fruit whose mortal taste brought death into the world and all out woe. A waiter once confided the trouble, which it seems is terminological. An apple is a Table Apple.

* * *

LITTLE SAROYAN, HOW DO YOU DO?

Statistical Prefactory

I wrote "The Time of My Life" in three hours and eight minutes not counting a telephone call; it wasn't for me, but wait. After this play is produced I will have to have five or six secretaries who do nothing but answer the telephone. "No, he can't be disturbed." "No, he has no open date for four months."

Getting a title for this play was easy. I will tell you how it happened. In the room where I wrote this play, and I will tell where it is in good time, because people will want to make pilgrimages there, the way they do to Stratford, well, in this room there was a copy of "Time" and one of "Life," although I do not know Henry Luce at all. I feel sorry for, have a compassion for, William Shakespeare, though his initials also were fortunately starred.

Good as "The Time of My Life" is, I feel that it is only a foretaste of what is to come—a curtain-raiser to the rest of my career.

During the writing of this play I smoked two packages of Sweet Caporal cigarettes; and eleven White Owl cigars, using a lot of matches, which, like a fool, I forgot to count. Once for five minutes I became so absorbed in the writing of "The Time of My Life" that I almost forgot myself. This will not happen again if I can help it.

I figure that people will advertise my play in ordinary conversation. How many times have you heard people say "I had the time of my life"? Do you ever hear people say "Hamlet" or "Tobacco Road"?

"The Time of My Life" will be the American theater's only important play until my next one is written. Probably in five years no other plays but mine will be produced in America. Suppose I take as much as four weeks to write a play, that's 13 plays a year 65 plays in 5 years. Theaters will have to be built; countless laborers will get jobs. Thus I am a public benefactor, too.

ACT 1

The Place

A typical second-rate saloon, such as you have seen a thousand times in West Superior, Wis., though this place of Joe's happens to be in New York, near the East River, a little north of Brooklyn Bridge. On the bar is a container, white with maroon stripes, holding stale popcorn. It is covered by a screen, to keep the flies off. Nobody on the stage ever takes any popcorn, though in Act III a man named Cooper lifts the screen, looks at the popcorn, and then puts the screen back.

JOE, a man who is 41 years, 4 months and 8 days old, though he looks a little younger, is standing behind the bar. He is bartender and proprietor. FRED, a man of approximately the same age, is standing at the bar, looking a trifle irresolute.

FRED—Morning, Joe.

JOE—Isn't morning. It's (*he consults a silver watch from his pants pocket*) about eight past two.

FRED—It's an old habit of mine. Used to work on a morning paper. Came to work one, two in the afternoon. Seems like morning always till about night time.

Joe—Is that so?

Fred—Sure. You know that.

Joe—I know I do. But got to say something until somebody else comes in. Then you and him can talk.

Fred—You and *he*. Excuse me. Used to work on a copydesk, you know, correct what reporters write. Had to correct sloppy talk like yours.

Joe—Say, if you don't like my talk, you can go where you got to put your nickel on the line instead of rolling up credit with a bad talker. You owe me 65c now.

Fred—Now Joe. Only kidding. How about a beer?

Joe—O. K. That's 70c.

Fred—Here's a quarter. Deduct.

Joe—O. K. Now you owe me 45c.

(*Enter Gertrude, a young woman of 24. She is vital and sweet.*)

Gertrude—Pardon me, but may I use your telephone?

Joe—Sure. I mean surely. In there (*He points*).

Gertrude—Pardon me, but might I bother you for two nickels for a dime?

Joe—Surely. Certainly, madam. (*Gives her two nickels; she hands him a dime.*)

Fred—I wish I had a nickel to give you. I'm a poor man. (*Sings*) "When a poor man came in sight, gathering winter fu-u-el,"

Gertrude—Here's a dollar. Go buy yourself some coal and wood, my friend.

Fred—Thank you.

Gertrude—You're welcome. You look like a man who has had more fortunate times.

Fred—I am. (*Sings*)

> "Some poor old mother is waiting
> for her,
> "Who has seen better days."

Hell, are you going to telephone? Answer yes or no.

GERTRUDE—Hell, no. I was going to telephone a friend of mine, Stephen H. Merriwether, but you're my friend now.

(*Enter Newsboy*).

NEWSBOY—Paper?

GERTRUDE—No, thanks.

NEWSBOY (to Joe)—Paper?

JOE—No.

NEWSBOY (to Fred)—Paper?

FRED—No.

(*Exit Newsboy.*)

GERTRUDE—Will you have a drink, my new friend?

FRED—Thanks, I don't care if I do. Joe, a whisky sour.

GERTRUDE—Same for me.

FRED—I like whisky sours. Hell, maybe the plural is whiskies sour. Gets you down, things like that.

GERTRUDE—They're good drinks, anyway.

JOE—Two whisky sours.

(*They drink, looking at each other. The telephone rings.*) Excuse me, while I answer. (*Goes to telephone.*) Hello. Yes. Joe. No, I don't know. He ain't been in today. Yop, I'll tell him.

(*Enter Mr. Clarkson, a well-dressed man of about 37 years of age*) Oh, Mr. Clarkson. A lady just telephoned. No message. Said she'd call again at the beginning of the second act. Want to wait?

CLARKSON—Yes. It's only a minute or two. That's like Alice, though. Give me a drink (*Notices the others*). I'll have a whisky sour. Won't you two have something?

GERTRUDE—Thank you, I'll have a whisky sour.

FRED—Same here.

* * *

THE DIARY OF OUR OWN
SAMUEL PEPYS

Wednesday, February 6, 1935

This day I heard, and only this day, that there is a strong likelihood that at Harvard University the requirement of Latin for the degree of Bachelor of Arts will be eliminated, and that in order to improve the status of the Bachelor of Science. It seems to me that that way madness lies, especially if education be a goal. For whilst I well know that there do be many men whom I do consider to be educated, although they may have taken courses in Latin for six or eight years, I do not hold that a man is educated without any study of Latin soever. And I wonder what has happened at Yale since that school jettisoned the study of Latin from its requirements for the Arts degree. But this morning I met a young woman whose employer is a Harvard alumnus, and I said, What does your employer think about the dropping of Latin, and she said that she did not know, but that she thought it was well dropped, and I asked her whether she ever had studied any Latin soever, and she said, I should say not. So all day at the office, after an irksome hour at the dentist's, and so home and worked, and my boy had a postal card from his mother, with a picture of Rip Van Winkle's house, and a message, "Tell Papa to tell you the story," and I looked for it, to read it to him, and not a volume of Washington Irving in my house, and I wondered how many such houses there were these days. But I told him the tayle, including the drunkenness.

Friday, February 15

Up, and read about Hilaire Belloc, who came to this country yesterday, and how he said that of all the things he had wrote, his verse alone was what he liked. And his verse alone is what of his I like. And I do not doubt that of all the persons who write both verse and prose, the verse is what they like, and what most of their readers like. For it is what remains, as a rule, in the memory; and therefore has a better chance with posterity. Lord! I can recall many of Mr. Belloc's verses, like:

> When I am dead, I hope it may be said:
> "His sins were scarlet, but his books were read."

And:

> The Tiger, on the other hand, is kittenish and mild;
> He makes a pretty playfellow for any little child;
> And the mothers of large families (who claim to common sense)
> Will find a Tiger well repay the trouble and expense.

So to the office, where all day and so home for a little, and so to Alice Miller's for supper, very hopeful and light-hearted.

Saturday, February 16

Betimes up, and to my office, and thence by train to New Haven, and in the evening with my wife to see "The Gondoliers," and I did marvel again at Miss Muriel Dickson's to sing so well "Kind sir, you cannot have the heart." And I found what Mr. G. B. Shaw wrote for the London World on October 11, 1893, though the opera that he was considering was "Utopia." "But people who are not musicians," he wrote, "should not intrude into opera houses; indeed, it is to me an open question whether they ought to be allowed to exist at all. As to the score generally, I have only one fault to find with Sir Arthur's luxurious ingenuity in finding pretty timbres of all sorts, and that is that it still leads him to abuse the human voice unmercifully. I will say nothing about the part he has written for the unfortunate soprano, who might as well leave her lower octave at home for all the relief she gets from the use of her upper one. A composer who uses up young voices by harping on the prettiest notes in them is an ogreish voluptuary; and if Sir Arthur does not wish posterity either to see the stage whitened with the bones of his victims or else to have his music transposed wholesale, as Lasalle transposes Rigoletto, he should make up his mind whether he means to write for a tenor or a baritone, and place the part accordingly. . . . The book has Mr. Gilbert's lighter qualities without his faults." So to a publick for some oysters, and so to bed.

Wednesday, February 27

Four years ago this day the New York World ceased to be, and I may yet turn into a pillar of salt on one of these anniversaries. So finished reading what I thought an over-repetitious book, "Call It Sleep," and by coincidence read an editorial in the Saturday Review of Literature, "Battle of the Books," which took the words out of my mouth. For it says that most of the novels are too long, though there is no arguing, it says, with masterpieces. "But it was genius, not length that did it," it says. And I would add that I do read a masterpiece in spite of its length. And it says:

> For it is our reasoned opinion that ninety-nine novels out of a hundred could be cut from one-quarter to a third with positive gain. That in ninety novels out of a hundred excessive length is due to the unwillingness or inability of the writer to control his imagination and the medium in which he works. The eighty long novels out of a hundred are nothing but short novels puffed up, padded out, stretched by the insertion of a mass of undigested material from the lazy brain of the writer, who has not taken time to work its essence into his story. . . . Good

fiction is good prose, which, heaven knows, most modern novels in English are not.

It is, I think, a lack of self-discipline that these verbose writers have. They write their books perhaps one-third too long; the third that might profitably be deleted took a long time to write; pride of authorship, the feeling that all that time and trouble seems wasted may keep them from throwing that third away. What "Battle of the Books" says is better said, often enough, by Mr. James Hughes, who hath the privilege of putting my sayings into type. "This is awful long," he says. "You must have been in a hurry." So home and then to supper with H. McGee and K. Campbell, and pretty early home and to bed.

Friday, March 8

Read more in T. Wolfe's "Of Time and the River," and there is in it almost everything; to my notion too much, and in too, too many words. It is plain that Mr. Wolfe must suffer deeply the wrongs and injustices of the world, but I think he could do better if he could discipline himself to write less repetitiously, and not be so carried away, as he seemeth to be, by the sound of his voice, which, in writing leads to lyricitis. But Lord! what a colossal book, with what a mixture of balderdash and grandeur, of bathos and heartbreak, of heavy-handed humour and bitter and furious satire!

Saturday, March 9

Last night and this morning I did read more in "Of Time and the River," and did marvel at the mere industriousness and patience of setting down all those 912 pages of words, but marveled even more of the quality in T. Wolfe, as I do see it, that seemingly makes him unable to elide many of the pages. For an idea of what I call his wordiness I do get from his dedication, which some writers might make "To Max Perkins" and let it go at that, but which Mr. Wolfe doeth thus:

To

MAXWELL EVARTS PERKINS

A great editor and a brave and honest man, who stuck to the writer of this book through times of bitter hopelessness and doubt and would not let him give in to his own despair, a work to be known as "Of Time and the River" is dedicated with the hope that all of it may be in some way worthy of the loyal devotion and the patient care which a daunt-less and unshaken friend has given to each part of it, and without which none of it could have been written.

So it being a fine day, I at home and all the day at work until after six, and so I out to dinner with J. Toohey, he telling me tayles of "Rain," and of Miss Bankhead, whom I should like to ask what hath become of her old friend Jobyna Howland. So to catch up H. Benedict, and so to join some cronies at a card game, my fortune being as ill as might be.

Monday, March 11

Up, and to the dentist's, great fun, and so to my office, as delightful a place as any ever I worked in, and so home, and after a joyous dinner fell to discussing things with my wife, and she said she was wearied of reading that writing was a difficult trade, or that there were obstacles in the way of its smooth accomplishment. She right, as always she is, so I vowed to omit in future all allusions to aught but ways of pleasantness and paths of peace. So to bed, mighty merry, and so anxious for the next day to begin, so that I might be at my ineffably lovely work again that I barely could sleep at all, what with the happiness of anticipation.

Wednesday, March 13

Woke, far happier than I was eighteen years ago this day, when first I set foot in France, at Le Havre, having crossed in the not so good, but crowded ship Londonderry from Southampton. Mighty wroth at the news from Chicago that Mr. John Evelyn Strachey is so revolutionary a speaker, and holds such naughty opinions, that our government he would break down. Yet when some orator quotes Thomas Jefferson that all men are created equal there is great cheering, from those who would say, "This country, based upon the principle of freedom, allows freedom of expression to its citizens and to the strangers within its gates." Also it seemeth to me that what a man espouseth will be adopted generally if it be good; and if it be bad it will be rejected. So what difference is it what this or that one hath to say? So to the office, and all the day there, in great good humour at the ease with which words fell together, and that some of them made sense.

Friday, March 15

This day the Ides, but I enthralled by my work, and over-joyed at paying my income tax to the darling Collector. So with my wife to see "Life Begins at 8:40."

Friday, March 22

Up, of a springlike morning, and worried about the increasing acuteness of the notes between Germany and any other nation; and deeply concerned over the number of newspapers and persons who say that there cannot possibly be any war. So read about the funeral of Louis Wiley, and remembered well how romantic he was about journalism, and how 15 yrs. ago he sighed for the days when a morning paper was a morning paper, and not something that could be bought on the street at nine in the evening.

Monday, March 25

Up, and read a mighty good article in Harper's, by Isabelle Keating, called "Reporters Come of Age," mostly about the Newspaper Guild, whose formation I clamoured for in 1912. And she says, in saying that the Guild has not moved with legalistic stealth or caution or indeed with much diplomacy, "And this is because newspaper men and women do not act that way. A man who has been taught to ask the mayor whether he stole the city's $50,000 or the latest police prisoner whether he really murdered the little girl after he kidnaped her is a believer both by instinct and training in direct methods." True; and oddly enough a newspaper man is accustomed to being believed, especially by his editors, and he is not instinctively given to over-statement. As to diplomacy, he has seen so much of it, and so much of it done by what he would call hypocrites and liars, that he hates the very name of it, and often leans to overbluntness.

Saturday, May 18

Early wakened by my boys, one saying "Don't make so much noise; he said that he wanted to sleep this morning," and the other saying, "I am not making noise; I'm quieter than you are," and then many exchanges of "You are not" and "I am, too." And then one called "I'm a hundred times as quiet as you are," and the other saying, "I'm fifty katrillion times as quiet as you are." And if it had been nations talking, one saying, "I'm more peaceful than you are," the world might well have been embroiled in war.

Monday, June 3

My wife telephones me that Tim will come to the country the morrow morn, which I am glad of, as all of my children will then be here, and I taking care of them instead of doing other even more irksome work. Last week came to see me Wm. L. White, whom I had not seen since he was a Harvard student, and tells me he is now thirty-five yrs. of age, and is seeking employment of a journalistick nature in this city, forasmuch as Emporia is too easy and familiar to him. And yesterday Mr. Rob Duffus wrote a piece in the Times about W. A. White, Bill's father, wherein W. A. said that young Bill wrote most of the editorials in the Emporia Gazette, and that the old man got credit for most of them, and that, I think, would be reason enough for a boy to want to move away. So to work this morning and all afternoon, too, and in the evening pretty early to bed.

Saturday, June 29

This morning early up, and to my office, which I have a notion to rechristen by breaking a bottle of ink over it and calling it the I Used To Be Alone; for I make either so good a mousetrap or poem that my children, all of whom can now walk, but all of whom never walk but always run, that the world of children beat a path to my door. So all the morning at work; and in the afternoon with my wife to W. Sachs's, in Darien, and played nothing but doubles, save one set of singles, but with my wife. Which recalled how George Gershwin's father, having promised George that he would eschew his nightly pinochle games that kept him out so late, did come home on the first night of his vow after 1 in the morning. So George charged him with having broken his

promise, but Mr. Gershwin said, "But I was playing with
my cousin." So to dinner, and then Emanie asked me for a
title for a history of Kentucky, but I could think of nothing
but "Weep No More." But on the way home I thought of
another—"My Old Kentucky Home, Good Night!"

Monday, September 23

Up early, and to the city by train, and read with great
glee that there will be a world's fair here in 1939, and that
it will be in a park to be laid out at Flushing; and I thought
that the first controversy would be concerning who originated
the idea, albeit there is a chance that before it is at an end
the controversy will be who shall be blamed for it. And that
it will be even greater than the fair that was held in Chicago
in 1893 I make no doubt, although there will be no Puck
Building, and no Sousa's Band and no Theodore Thomas
orchestra. Great talk about the peace proposals, and Mussolini and Ethiopia; and there are ancestral headlines
prophesying war; but the stories under these headlines seem
far less martial. Yet it strikes me that Mussolini feels that
he will dislike whatever the proposals are. So all the day so
hard at work that I was put to it to catch the late train, and
it was dark when I got home, and went early to bed.

Wednesday, October 9

Early up, and by train to the city and to the office, and
read that little Carleton Nichols had been expelled from the
school in Lynn for his refusal to salute the flag, and things
are like that in Saugus, too, where three little children said
that their religious beliefs would not permit them to salute
the flag. And their mother, who is a member of a sect called
Jehovah's Witnesses, said that she could not give allegiance
to the flag because that would be putting Jehovah second.
So I thought that the Daughters of the Revolution ought to

expel Ethan Allen, who asked for Fort Ticonderoga to surrender in the name of "the Great Jehovah and the Continental Congress." And the Loyal Sons of This-or-That ought to refuse to let their sons attend the university at New Haven, forasmuch as their song is not only sung to the air of "Die Wacht am Rhein," but also it puts the nation in second place in "For God, for country, and for Yale." Nor is country capitalized. So even on the same page I saw that a Mr. James Doran would like the newspapers to refrain from printing liquor advertisements in their Sunday issues; and that the Mayor had ordered that everybody in the city administration who had any political post should resign from that post. And it seems that the whole world is being its brother's keeper; or being in the attitude of "See what Johnny is doing and tell him not to do it."

Sunday, October 20

Finished reading S. Lewis's "It Can't Happen Here," and whilst I was reading it I felt that this or that passage was too long, but after I finished I found that the cumulative effect was tremendous, and the book imagines what might happen in this land if a dictator were President, or rather if the President were a dictator, and it is not so fantastic as it might be, neither. And it seems to me that not only could It Happen Here, but also that more of it is happening here than many of us are conscious of. Now when Mr. H. G. Wells pictures what might happen a hundred years from now I find it hard to read, and I do not think that ten of his books of that sort are worth one "Tono Bungay" or "The History of Mr. Polly." But I think that this book of Lewis's outweighs his pure fiction. That he is no deep student of Communism or Fascism is, I think, an asset to him. For he is a terrific patriot, and cries and screams aloud that his country is menaced by the things and the persons he hates.

And it heartens me to think that there is somebody who still has the capacity for indignation, and has not grown tired of getting angry, like most of us weary cowards who say, discouraged, "What is the use?"

Tuesday, November 5

To my office early, it being Election Day in this city, and Guy Fawkes Day in England, and one meaning as much to me as another, which is nothing. So thought I would write a piece called

SYSTEM

Every day my stuff I do
And work as hard as you or you;
And every day when I don't shirk
I get a cocktail after work,

which reminded me to go to A. Kober's drinking party, but I drank not at all, to am't to anything, and so home, and with my wife to see "Pride and Prejudice," a play made from the novel, and I felt unique in that I never had read the novel, and of twenty persons I asked about it Alice Miller was the only one who had read it, but her escort, Mr. Marx the harpist, said that he may have read it; that it may have been the book he read. So to G. Kaufman's to a great party, and had a merry time there, and Miss Fontanne there, and she suffered me to kiss her, saying, "Goody! goody!" which I considered the high point in her histrionism. So talked with Margalo Gillmore and Emma Ives and so waited for my wife to say good by, and I said "Come on home, Adelina Patti," which was a mild allusion to the many farewell performances that that singer gave. So home and to bed, a little past two in the morning.

Sunday, November 10

Lay till after eight, and so up and indulged in some Narcissism, and so did some work, but had a feeling that nothing that I could do would be good enough, and after dinner to the office and thence home the rest of the day, casting up accounts and paying so many bills that it depleted my check book, for which I was mighty glad, albeit my wife tells me that she would give me some checks on another bank, and I might cross the name of it off, which I told her was a kindness I did not know what I had done to deserve. So listened to the Town Crier tell about the war, and felt that he still is too sentimental about that silly, boring, rotten conflict that made nothing safe for democracy, nor was a war to end wars.

Sunday, November 17

Early up and to the village to get a newspaper, and so home and read it, and thence to Bronxville to Dot Lewis's, and a great crowd there, and a stimulating one. And Herbert Wells gave me a cigar, and a good one, and he tells me that he thinks that the motion pictures will eventually be the greatest expression of art, but I do not think so, forasmuch as by the time the cinema is in charge of persons who are as intelligent and uncensorable as the publishers of newspapers and books, there will be some art and some method of expression that will make the cinema look ancient. So met Miss G. B. Stern, a grandly humorous girl, and talked with her about letters; and then there was talk about fascism, and Mr. Wells thought that it could not happen here, but Geo. Seldes and Bob Forsythe heckled Mr. Wells a good deal, they feeling that the nation was well on its way to it. Lord! I think that there is no way of comparing this nation to any European nation, and that the greatest foe of fascism, and of communism, too, is geography. But all the talk mighty good to hear, though the obbligato of Father Coughlin's bombast over the radio diverted my attention. So Mrs. Alice Longworth drove me home in a fine petrol-carre, and so had supper, and went early to bed.

Thursday, November 28

Early up, and of a warm Thanksgiving morning to the village to get the newspapers, and read Mr. Hoover's address, made yesterday in San Francisco. "The woof of our form of society," he said, "was woven into the warp of liberty at the Revolution." Now I think that that is a technical, if not a high-brow expression; forasmuch as I asked many non-weavers what a woof was, and a warp; and nobody knew, and without looking it up I can not remember which is the lengthwise thread and which the crosswise; but I think the warp is the lengthwise, because in the usual form it comes first. And Lord! what difference there is between the Revolution and the revolution; perhaps a difference not only in capitalization, but also in tense. News come that on the sands at Southampton a man had found an elongated fish, and the conundrum is what is the difference between that and the Administration's program? One is a dune eel.

Monday, December 2

Mighty betimes up, and away to the office I went, and was there all day, what with many visitors coming to my office. So on the way home I thought how Belle Hardwick, leaving her husband in the Wayne house, where much interesting matter was about to happen, left with regret, saying "And to think that I've only got Tom to describe it to me! I wish I'd married Graham McNamee," and how my wife nudged me, saying "I know just how she feels." And that all wives felt like that, their husbands being laconic, though I think that non-volubility is a good fault. But I told her that husbands had no such complaint, most of us being married to the feminine of Graham McNamee. Yet Graham, for all I know, is a taciturn fellow at home. But when I reached home I said "Friends, I left the office of the New York Herald Tribune, 230 West Forty-first Street, New York, at 5:43, Perpetual Self-Winding Watch time, taking the northermost elevator. I entered the Interborough Rapid Transit Company's station at Forty-first Street, occupying a seat in a car that was second from the front. The car, not the seat. Ha ha. There were thirty-seven persons in the car, twenty women and seventeen men. The first woman I noticed was about forty-one years of age; she was wearing a black coat with black fur collar, black half shoes, and beige stockings. Sorry, but my time is up. Tomorrow evening at the same time. You have been listening to the voice of Papa." "Oh," said my wife, "I wouldn't be too certain of that." So to dinner, and by nine o'clock to bed.

Thursday, December 5

Very gayly up, and read Donald Robert Perry Marquis's "archy does his part," very good, nor did I like anything in it better than the poem on the navy being in town that was printed in this journal. But what a deeply humorous man Don is, and far closer to Mark Twain than anybody I know and am likely ever to know. So to the office and home at four, and in the evening out to play at cards with some young cronies, and lucky ones too, and so home at some godly hour, and to bed.

Friday, December 13

Early up, and to school with my daughter, she saying "Good morning" to everybody on the way, and saying to me "I have nine friends." Which is, to my notion, a great number. If she never becomes a newspaper writer, she may always have as many as nine friends. So to the office, and sorrowed to read about the chances of peace between Ethiopia and Italy, and I think that the only thing that will please both is to have France, Great Britain, the United States, China, and Japan all at war, and if with one another, so much the better. It is a sad and silly world, but I no longer think that it is my messianic task to make it gay and wise.

Tuesday, December 31

To work before nine o'clock, very hard, and finished my stint by one in the afternoon. So ends the year, I glad of seeing it go. For I have had moments of great happiness in it, but days of woe and sadness. The world is in sorry state, I think, the League of Nations being of none more effect upon the waging of war than the defunct Federal League. The President is in disfavour with many, but in favour with enough voters, I feel certain, to gain his office again. And some say this man will oppose him, and some say that; but I think that Governor Landon will oppose him. That the country is in far better a condition of prosperity than it was last year this day there is no doubt; but some say that it is the President's fault, and some say that the nation is like the patient who would get well in spite of a malpracticing doctor. Mr. Al Smith hath said Nay to an invitation to stay the night at the White House; and I wish I might read what is in the Roosevelt and the Smith mind. For maybe the President thought "It would be good politics to invite Mr. Smith," and maybe Mr. Smith thought that it would be good politics not to accept. But I think that Mr. Smith never forgave Mr. Roosevelt for getting the nomination in 1932; and a mighty human feeling, too. So in the evening caught up Patty Waldron, and drove her to Ralph Boyer's, and had a bottle of French champagne, and so home by eleven, my wife driving me.

Sunday, January 19, 1936

Yesterday I read that Rudyard Kipling had died, and it saddened me, as he was a great influence on millions of readers, and for that matter on non-readers. And a tremendous influence on writers, many of whom would not ever know that he was an influence on them. For in many ways he was a trail-blazer, and it is a truth that those who ride along the smooth highway no longer remember the man but for whom there would be no road at all. And I am indignant against these critics and poets who speak condescendingly of Kipling as a mere balladist, or a journalist-poet. As though anybody at all could write a mere ballad! And so I was for writing a long piece of journalistic verse myself, which God knoweth is the only kind that I can write, and never yet have I seen a piece of verse or prose that I thought too good to print in a newspaper, as I have said many times, and feel more strongly about each year. So I set this down:

I scoff at those who call it prose, who chafe at the chains of
   rhyme,
Who think that they could have been R. K. if they'd only
   taken the time.
They've often hissed "Imperialist," and called him a bard
   of news;
I demand that they quit, for few are fit to shine the Kipling
   shoes.
The Kings depart, but the poet's heart beats until Time is
   through—
And he was a poet, a regular poet, poet and journalist too.

Sunday, January 26

This morning I did not awake till after nine o'clock, and so up and read Mr. Al Smith's speech that he made last night in Washington, and I was reminded how Mr. Clifton Fadiman had mentioned Mr. Smith as one of the politicians by whom I had been fooled. But Mr. Smith and I are older, and, much as I should like to be fooled by him, I am not. For I thought his words were based wholly on a hatred of the Roosevelt administration, which is not the tolerant attitude that I once thought was his. But I think that it also is unfair to assail him for having friends of great wealth, for that alone would no more condemn him than having friends of no wealth at all would make him great. And as for his having moved from No. 51 to No. 820 Fifth Avenue, I hold that of no importance, for the apartment that he had downtown was a beautiful and a spacious one, a penthouse with a solarium, and mighty costly, I will be bound. But when he lived there nobody flayed him for not still residing on Oliver Street. Lord! what surface things Hatred and Jealousy attack! And the basic things they apparently are blind to. So to my office, and on the way I was appalled by the snow piled with accumulated rubbish near the office, and told the editor about it, and he sent Mr. Zerbe the photographer to make a picture of it for tomorrow's newspaper. And I wish that some day he would take some photographs of the newsstands next to subway exists and entrances that make the sidewalk too narrow for pedestrian traffic. So home, and in the evening with A. Woollcott to dinner, and Neysa there, and Janet Flanner there, whom I have not seen in many years, and after dinner I took her home, and so I home and to bed, reading "In Dubious Battle," an engrossing tale of a strike in the California apple orchards, and of the men engaged in it.

Saturday, February 8

Lay long, and so up and to luncheon with A. Krock, and he tells me things about Washington, and the place is now so bewildering that I do not see how he, or anybody else, can select, from an embarrassment of poverty or richness, what single matter to select to write about. So in the afternoon to Capt. John Thomason's, and met there Commander Stone and his wife, a mighty knowing lady, and I told John that I thought so, and then he tells me that she is Grace Zaring Stone that wrote "The Bitter Tea of General Yen," and I was glad that I did not know it, and I remember a play of Chesterton's, I think it was "Magic," wherein somebody said that you never really know anybody if you know his name. So to catch up D. Taylor, and with him to dinner at the Press Club, and thenafter I sate next Mr. Jos. Byrnes the Speaker of the House, and listened to many long speeches, by H. Broun and A. Woollcott and D. Taylor, and thenafter there was dancing, and for all that I know, light wines, but I home and to bed.

Monday, February 10

Up, and about the town, here and there, and thence to the Supreme Court, at eleven, and heard much talk about the lack of dignity of the place, and how the old building was far worthier of the high tribunal, but I thought that this was still the most august and dignified place I ever had seen, and even if it were undignified, why, when the Court is so great a target, and some even want to have it abolished, should it be more dignified. Dignity is as dignity does, and there could be dignity in a composing room, and there could be none in the Senate. So to E. Lindley's for dinner, and early to bed.

Tuesday, February 11

Dashed about all the day, this being far different from the sheltered life I lead in my domestic hermitage. So to the White House, and met F. Roosevelt the President, who told me that he was glad to see me, and I was about to tell him that I hadn't known he cared, but thought that I would wait my opportunity, which did not come again. So to the office and worked a little, and thence to dinner at G. Pinchot's, and I sate next Mr. Burton Wheeler the Senator from Montana, and he told me that he was at Ann Arbor just after I had left, though he never had thought of it in that way before. But though he lives in Butte, he was born in Hudson, Mass., and lived there for a long time. But there was one thing that I did not ask him: and that was whether he knew Myron Brinig and Berton Braley, the Butte litterateurs.

Thursday, February 13

Out, into the iciest, slipperiest morning ever I experienced, and so to the office at eleven, but nobody yet there, so I could not enter, and so went to see P. Oehser at the Smithsonian Institution, and mighty much interested in some of it, but not the natural history portion. But I will be bound that there are thousands of Americans who have visited the museums and galleries of France and Italy who would scorn to go to the Smithsonian, yet were the same thing in these foreign lands they would not dare to come home and say that they had not seen it, yet would be the first to scream about the Constitution, and down with the traitor and up with the star. So to call upon Mr. Schuyler Merritt who represents, among other towns, Lyons Plain; and a fine representative gentleman, too. And he gave me a luncheon, of oysters and bluefish; and so I to the office and put down

too many words, none much good, and so to pack my grip-
sack; and so downstairs to see Hazel Vandenberg, and found
Arthur there, and said Lord! how did you get home so early
after speaking in New York last night? And he said he came
home on the night train, but that he got the early editions
of the morning papers to see how his speech looked in print.
Which I thought a mighty engaging admission, and I told
him that I had my November telegram already composed,
and he asked me what it was, and I told him "Better luck
next time." And his merriment was sincere. So to catch up
Mrs. Alice Longworth and with her to see G. Cohan in
"Dear Old Darling," a small play save for the almost
incredibly fine acting of Mr. Cohan, and never have I seen
so authentick a bit of intoxication portrayed. So to the train
for home, and fell asleep before ever the train had left the
station.

Thursday, February 20

Lots of silly talk about whether Walter Johnson will be
able to throw a silver dollar across the Rappahannock River,
as George Washington is said to have done, albeit there
were no dollars until after Washington had died. But why
did all of us think that it was the Potomac? And I recalled
the time Joe Weber said that he knew of a man who could
throw a ball five thousand yards. "It's possible," said
Fields. "It's impossible," said Weber, "I seen it myself."
"Who could do such a thing?" asked Fields. "That was
your brother," said Weber. "Oh," said Fields, "*he* could
do it." And I wondered whether I could throw a dollar
across the Saugatuck; but I would not if I could, but would
throw it from Lyons Plain into Mr. Sniffen's bank. And as
to Sol Bloom betting twenty to one against Walter Johnson,
I would bet a silver dollar that not a cent changes hands. So
to the office, one and all saying how fine I looked, and I said,

Well, if I get enough sleep I always look fine. And one and all said, Did we ever invite you to stay up? And I had to confess none had. So home and Mabel come for supper, and thenafter she and my wife exchanged their girlish confidences, and I fell asleep at nine o'clock.

Monday, March 2

Yesterday morning the workers in many edifices in the city, members of the Building Service Employees Union, decided to cease work, they desiring to work fewer hours per diem, and to receive more money—the desire of every human being. Lord! my wish is to have a great wage for not working at all, and why those who dislike to read what I write, or even to live in a world wherein such matter is printed, do not form a union to pay me as much for not writing as I can earn by writing. Hypocrites all, I say. But this high sounding name of Building Service Employees are the men who run the lifts and put coal on the furnace, and in some buildings the men who stand at doors, and whistle to a taxidriver who already is at the door. Now the Mayor is right when he says that such a strike would be inimical to the city's health. But how any union can get anything from any employers unless what they do is not only essential to the business of the employers but also when it is necessary to the health and comfort of the publick. For then, if the demands of the union seem just, the publick sympathizes with the workers. Now if there were a strike of blue-feather-on-women's-hat stickers nobody would be much inconvenienced by such a strike, and I doubt even whether the news of it would be printed in the newspapers. Nor is there much said in the press hereabout about the strike of the Hearst employees in Milwaukee, rebelling against what they call low pay and long hours and bad conditions of work. News this morning that a myriad (10,000) Ethiopians had perished in northern Tembien. But there could be 10,000 a day perish in war which now is geographically remote from us, and it would not have the interest for us that this strike of the liftmen has. Perhaps the denizens in Tudor City soon will have literally to walk not only to work, but all the way downstairs to the sidewalk. G. Root to dinner, and did a card trick, which he taught to my boy, and I remembered that John Milholland told me that he started his career of magic by having learned a trick from Kellar, and I thought how haply in a year or two I might be able to retire, and wondered what work the parents of Shirley Temple do.

Friday, March 13

Up at seven, and read of the things that are happening in Europe, how four Locarno powers, Great Britain, Italy, Belgium, and France, had found that the remilitarization of the Rhineland was a violation of the Locarno and Versailles treaties; and booh to you, pooh-pooh to you is what Hitler says, it seemeth to me. Yet every one of these powers, Germany included, will say that all that they want is peace. And it reminds me of nothing so much as the "Thar She Blows" legend; forasmuch as all they want is peace, and very little of that. So decided that Friday the Thirteenth was nought but a silly superstition; and so by the beautiful new Sixth Avenue Bus to the office; and was about to take train for the country, but the printermen had had too much other work to set my little article, so I must wait till afternoon. So Bess Toms tells me of a theater in Brooklyn, whose outer walls carry the legend "Ars longa Vita brevis est," and this day hath a film play therein called "Hitch-hike to Heaven." But Lord! with the lift strike many of us were glad to hitch-hike to the eleventh floor, which is as far away from Heaven as when I was a boy, as Tom Hood hath it. So hied to the train, and so home.

Monday, March 23

Up, but not very early, and Dorothy and I by motor-carre to the office, and so hard at work all day, and read about the six-year naval treaty of Great Britain, France and the United States; and one was that the maximum of capital ships is to be 35,000 tons; and that caused me to look up things about Sam'l Pepys and the British Navy; and when he first was associated with the Admiralty the battle-line was thirty ships, and the total tonnage was about 25,000; and when he left office twenty-eight years later, the total was fifty-nine ships of 66,000 tons. Lord! Mr. Pepys is best known for his Diary, and Dr. Oliver Wendell Holmes for his poems and breakfast-table essays, but it is the British Navy that is Pepys's monument, as it is obstetrics, especially in the reduction of maternal mortality, that is Dr. Holmes's. Though there are many who still think that his immortality rests upon the fame of his son that was Mr. Justice Holmes. So at this and that all day, and on the train heard some men discussing the allegiance of Dr. Townsend to Senator Borah, and I wonder how Mr. Borah likes that fealty. But I think that it will do him no good. Mr. Borah I heard last night over the wireless, but it seemed to me that if I had not known who was speaking I could not have told, save that it was not the President, for say what you will about him, but not I pray, you to me, save it be short, he speaks the speech tripplingly on the tongue. So home, and to supper, and early to bed.

Tuesday, March 24

Up very early, and to the station, and met there Mike Williams the pamphleteer, and I upbraided him for being a neighbour of mine, though he dwells a ten-mile span from me, for not coming to visit me; and he tells me many things, but I forgot to ask him why I no longer get The Commonweal. So rode on the train with Florence Clisbee, and we solved the crossword puzzle in a few minutes, but she is more adroit and patient than I, forasmuch as her first duty is to solve the cryptograms appearing on the penultimate page of the Herald Tribune. So to the office, and all day there, at many duties, and hearing that because of Mussolini's nationalization of Italy's industries, stocks in Italy had decreased in value. And I wondered whether there would be a learned financial article, called "The Decline and Fall of the Roman Stock Market." So in the afternoon about the town on literary business, and so to dinner, and thenafter with my wife to see Rob Sherwood's "Idiot's Delight," which I not only enjoyed better than any of his other plays, but felt that it was good, and would do more for the cause of peace and against the cause of war than plays written and played in the blinding heat of propaganda, and Mr. Lunt and Miss Fontanne so good that it seemed that nobody could be any better, and that is how it seemed to me about them all, from Miss Jacqueline Page and Mr. Richard Whorf, who is the most versatile actor ever I saw, to Mr. Bretagne Windust and Mr. Sydney Greenstreet. My only fear about the import of the play is that most of the talk about it will be about Mr. Lunt's song-and-dance act instead of the poignant import of the play; yet perhaps that is just as well, for when people think there is a lesson or a moral in the playhouse they fear to go. Lord! I think this Sherwood is a passionate, bitter fellow! So to a party at Alice Guinzburg's and had a pleasant time talking to Mrs. Lord; and so home at two in the morning.

Wednesday, May 6

Up at half past six, the smell of the country so fresh and sweet that I almost forgot about the snow and ice of yesterwinter. So up, and to the 7:38, and to the city, and so to my office, and read that B. Mussolini said that the war was finished, many Ethiopians having been butchered to make a Roman holiday. But as to the war being finished, that is what everybody said on November 11, 1918. But peace, as now we know, hath her battles no less renowned than war. News from California is that Mr. Landon hath lost the Presidential primary, and from many a headline it seems that the Democratic primary was nought, but the Roosevelt vote seemed to be large. But as to the defeat of Mr. Landon in California, I would not invade the privacy of anybody to say that the defeat may not have been wholly Landon's.

Wednesday, June 24

Early up and to breakfast with Mabel again, and so to the office, and found in an old newspaper, of 1932, what I had said about the Roosevelt candidacy, that at last there was a candidate younger than I, and how my wife had said it showed what comes of never giving up, and that is true, forasmuch as both parties have candidates younger than I. So now I have done better, and in only four years, and am a better model for Mr. Webster's Boy Who Made Good. All the day at the office, and so to supper with A. Goodrich and R. Kirby, and we were for going to see the films of the contest in the Roped Arena, and were told that it would be at nine o'clock, and we went to the theater, and went in, and they told us that it would not be until eleven, but that, said we, was past our bedtime, so we engaged in a brief cue tilt, and then F. Sullivan come along with two of his cronies, McKelway and Bryan, which sounded like 1896. But Mr. M. told me that he was mighty much taken with the sagacity of my political observations, which astounded me, forasmuch as I know nought about the subject, nor do I have much interest in it. And he said, that was just it, and I did not know whether to kiss him or to fell him with a blow, but refrained utterly. So home at eleven and to bed.

Saturday, June 27

Up and to my office, and so to the country, but it was a rainy day, so did nought but work all afternoon; and in the evening dawdled about until the Vice-President spoke, and he seemed to have a keen sense of humor, forasmuch as he spoke, or so it sounded to me, of Franklin Delaro Noosevelt, which was as comickall as anything said thus far in any convention held this year. And then the President himself spoke, and he spoke of what an old English judge said, and my wife said, "Now I suppose you are going to ask *what* English judge," and I said no, that I got tired of that the time he did not identify Josiah Royce. And when the musick preceding the advent of the President was announced it was called "Hail, all hail to the Chief," and I said that it was "Hail to the Chief who in triumph advances." And I asked her who wrote it, and she said "What difference does it make?" And I said "None, and it was Sir Walter Scott," but it was only a guess, and I am terrified to look it up. But as to phrases like Economic Royalists and such, and dictator-ships and such, the Republican party would say that it was opposed to such things, too. But the one good thing that he said was that governments may err and presidents makes mistakes; and the oftener he says such things the more he will seem like the common man who makes mistakes. But that a convention of this sort should have consumed five days is almost incredible.

Wednesday, July 1

Early up, and hastily at work, and at it all morning, and could not help wishing that I were an Economic Royalist, but the best that I could do was to sing it to "Fascinating

Rhythm." And I wondered whether the Mayor, Mr. La-
Guardia, who hath moved his headquarters to Pelham Bay
Park, may have done so because that neighborhood is
quieter than it is in City Hall Park, for even the Mayor is
powerless to suppress noise, and what hath become of all
this anti-noise business, when never an arrest or reprimand
do I hear of for a maker of superfluous noise, I do not know.
There is much prating about civic welfare and an abundant
life, but it seems to me that life in the city becometh daily
more exiguous. So after lunch drove Tim to Bridgeport, to
put him on the train for Camp Mooween, and so home and
did some more work, and in the evening to Kitty Jacobsen's,
in Ridgefield, to bid farewell to S. Chotzinoff against his
trip to Italy, and met there S. Howard, who tells me he hath
gone to Tyringham, Mass., to dwell; and Mr. Engle held
me with his glittering eye to tell me the iniquities of the
President, and how all artists and musicians like myself
were pro-Roosevelt because we had nothing to lose, but Lord!
a musician cannot play save that he be fed and clothed,
and that cannot be if nobody will pay to hear him.

Sunday, July 12

To Darien, to W. Sachs's, for luncheon and found there
Miss Frances Perkins, who told us many things about life
and labour and Washington; and she tells me that she thinks
that John Lewis is a mighty dramatic figure; but whether
he would win his fight for industrial unionism against Will
Green, and his fight against the steel owners she was in
doubt. But that Lewis, and Green, and the Iron and Steel
Institute, saying that they do not like dictatorship, yet
want to dictate. As who, desirous of power, does not? But
I should like to be dictated to once in a while, especially on
days when I am hard put to it to find something to have a
violent conviction about, and I want somebody to tell me

what to grow indignant about. So played two sets with W. Sachs, each winning one, and so stopped there for supper, and home then after, and to bed, reading Hillel Bernstein's "Choose a Bright Morning," a seemingly comick book, but full of meanings about the folly of the Mussolinis and the Hitlers, and what life under these humourless gentlemen is like.

Wednesday, July 15

Up at seven of St. Swithin's Day in the morning, and full of gaiety at my trip to the city, and met Dorothy Mason Ricker, and we talked about the time in 1926, when we drove from Auburn to Cortlandt, and went to a bookshop to ask whether there had been wide sales of "An American Tragedy," forasmuch as Chester Gillette, the Clyde Griffiths of the book, had worked there in his uncle's petticoat factory, and we asked the book salesman, and he said that he sold no copies whatsoever, and we asked him whether he knew anything about the case, and he said that Chester Gillette had been responsible for his having gone into the book business. And we asked him how, and he said that he had the job of sweeping out the factory, and that Gillette's uncle had fired him saying that he had to make a place for his nephew. And we asked him whether the factory still was there, and he said that the notoriety of the case, and also the dwindling demand for petticoats, had put the factory out of business. And we asked him whether "David Harum," which Cortlandt also was the scene of, had been a great seller in the town, and he said No. And so we called on a lady who had been identified with the case, who had married one of the attorneys in the case, and she was loath to speak of it, but later did, saying that she met Chester Gillette only at a dance, and then she answered the telephone, and it was her husband, and she said "Don't forget to bring home the hamburger for lunch." So to my office, cool and pleasant, and there all day at work, and so to dinner, of mackerel, albeit they tell me in Connecticut the mackerel are running low this season.

Tuesday, September 29

Very early up, and with my quartette of offspring to school, and left them all there, very happy. Now in the old days we were less overjoyed to go to school than are the children of today, and I think that is because people used to say to us, "Well, now you have to go to school again, and the pleasant vacation is all over," and now all the parents do not say those things to children, for one thing, and for another, the average school, publick or private, is far less irksome to youth than it used to be, though I confess that there were many things that I enjoyed about school, and was conscious at the time of enjoying them. And my greatest disappointment occurred on the night of February 12, 1892, when my parents would not let me go to a lecture on Abraham Lincoln at Central Music Hall, because of the blizzard, and I was a little interested in Lincoln, but much more in Hester Ridlon whom I would have sate next to. To the office, and home for supper, and to bed at nine o'clock.

Thursday, October 29

Up and without the curiosity or health to become interested in any of the political news, so to the office, and wrote my thoughts rapidly as I could, lest I should change my mind before I finished writing a Ballade of Passionate Indifference:

I am a lover of humankind;
Rapt am I at the daily show,
Caring who carves out Rosalind,
Wondering who's wherefixing Romeo.

But when I listen to those I know
Yelling and screaming and pulling hair about,
On account of a speech in Buffalo,
These are the things I do not care about.

All of them holler fortissimo;
All of their teeth they gnash and grind;
All of them promise a quid-pro-quo;
All of them promise the taxes low.
What do I care about who will row
The scow of state, or who turns her square about,
Hither and thither and to and fro?
These are the things I do not care about.

"Reds to Roosevelt are all inclined."
"Landon said not so long ago"—
"What, no Reds? You are color-blind."
"Farley says it's an overthrow."
"Hamilton says it's a ball of snow."
"Four years I am full of despair about."
"Wasting the taxpayers' precious dough."
These are the things I do not care about.

L'ENVOI

Prints, I'm a biased so-and-so;
There's not a thing I'm not unfair about.
Total the ballots, boys; although
These are the things I do not care about.

So in the evening began to listen to Mr. Landon's speech
over the air, but there was so much applause that when he
said "Mr. Chairman" ten times and they still cheered, I
thought that I have to strive harder than that to gain even
a single plaudit, and so to bed before ten o'clock.

Monday, November 2

Early up and to the office, and whilst I am glad that this is the last day of a campaign I am weary of, I think that the greatest relief will come to the reporters who have been not only listening to slight variants of the same speech for three months, but have been forced to write even slighter variants of the same story daily for three months, which I think is harder than making the speeches, forasmuch as much of the fervor that comes into a candidate's speech, whilst not necessarily assumed, becomes automatic; for I do not think that it is possible to be so continuously and articulately passionate about the principles of a party. And tomorrow the vote will not be cast by idolaters of Jefferson or of Lincoln, but by ordinary humanly selfish voters who feel that the candidate they vote for will make them richer or happier, or both. And if the people who voted for some other reason, and only those voted, the popular vote would be in the hundred thousands instead of in the forty-five millions. So in the evening to see "Forbidden Melody," as wearisome a musical play as I can recall having seen, and after the first act I met Miss L. Long and Rob Benchley, and it was five minutes to ten, and jests were passed about how it seemed to be four o'clock in the morning. So home and to bed.

Tuesday, December 1

This day I got Dorothy Parker's "No So Deep as a Well," and was moved to exaltation to find that the book had been laid at my feet, which may well be my more-enduring-than-brass monument. So to the office, and read that the King, if he marries Mrs. Simpson, might make her the Duchess of Cornwall, and she would then be known, I make so bold as to conjecture, as Lady Cornwallis. Mr. Valentine the police commissioner hath told detectives to put an end to the ridiculous begging business of watching motor cars; but nought will come of it, any more than of the talk about the freedom of the streets from parking; all streets being so cluttered up that one might say, with Field, "Fool that I was, I should have walked; I had no time to waste." So finished my stint, and so to the dentist's and thence home, and after a frugal supper, to bed.

Friday, December 11

Wakened this morning feeling that I had slept only a little and that it was the middle of the night, but found that it was a quarter past, or after, as they say in England, eight. Fell to wondering how many persons now would abdicate the King's English. So to the office, and met with Will Stevens the artist who tells me that Flossie Sheffield the West 10th Street Milk Horse no longer is attached to Sam's wagon, so I perturbed, and so called up Mr. Hess at the stables, who tells me Flossie is lame, but seems well enough in the morning but ill in the afternoon, and that she will not deliver 10th Street milk until she is utterly well. This day I do hear reviling of King Edward, that he is recreant, but I feel that he is a courageous fellow, and no coward at all; forasmuch as he seemeth to be a conscientious objector to panoply and hypocrisy. The Duke of York this day hath become King; and I did hear over the wireless the former King, as David Windsor, commend him to the people of the Empire. And his voice came clear and bold, and he ended with "God bless you all! God save the King!" mighty affecting.

Tuesday, December 15

Up, and to the office, and payed my income tax, which not only did not enrich the government much, but left me poor indeed. Yesterday was King George's birthday, and Mr. Stanley Baldwin said that no personal predilections will stand between him and what he conceives to be his first duty, and that is to fulfill his great task as King and Emperor. As who should say, "And this is what his elder brother did not do." Yet it is possible that Edward also did not let personal predilections stand between him and what he conceived to be his duty, which was to abdicate. And I think that no man should say that another man hath put this above that, and assume that he hath done wrong, for two men do not always have the same scale of values. But there is a great difference between the average man renouncing his job, and that of the abdication; forasmuch as when the average man renounces his job, he is without any money, or prospects of another job; and the Duke of Windsor, whatever betide, will be what even rich men would deem a wealthy man. All the day at my desk, and in the evening to bed an hour after supper.

Tuesday, December 22

This day the winter solstice comes, so I suspended work for a minute, from 1:37 to 1:38 this afternoon, and in the cause of candour, for an hour or two. So to the shops, to purchase some baubles for my boys, and I said, "Never mind wrapping them," and the saleswoman said, "You must think that you have an honest face, to walk out of Woolworth's with unwrapped packages," and I said, "What do you think?" And she gazed at me, and said, "Yes, you have." So home, and early to bed.

Wednesday, January 13, 1937

Lord! I grow aweary of a world of what seems to me needless hell. For there are murder and kidnaping here, and horror in Spain, and woe in Germany, and tyranny in Italy, and a great crash of an airplane near Los Angeles, killing passengers, and what causeth these planes to crash or to become uncontrollable I do not know, and it seems to me that as little cometh of these investigations as once came of train wrecks in which the engineer perished, and so the dead man was blamed for causing the wreck. The President hath recommended that there be two more Cabinet officers, one of Public Works and one of Social Welfare; and I am in favour of them, yet hope that nobody will tell me what is good for my social welfare, though I wish that there would be a Department of Telling Writers How to Write Five Hundred Words an Hour, so that I would not spend so many hours in staring ahead of me, or proofreading, and other matters in no wise connected with writing or the serenity needful for the reflection genius, not to say competency, must have. So lay pretty long, it seeming mighty hard to rise at all, and so to the office, and home early again and took a remedy which was a distillation made from pouring boiling water upon a grape fruit cut in eights, and as unpalatable a brew as ever I tasked, and had three such yesterday and today, and either on account of it or in spite of it I felt far less ill, and fell asleep before ten at night.

Thursday, January 21

Will Phelps is in Augusta, Georgia, gone from the wind and rain and snow, and he writes me that he saw in the New York Herald Tribune a note that Kennedy Brothers put a copy of "Gone With the Wind" on the shelves of their booth at the boat show, and that many came to ask whether it was a new yachting book; which I doubt, and I would like to know the names of three who seriously asked that question. But Will makes a pun and says that the yachters might have replied that it was having a good sale. But Wanamaker's once had a book called "Tobogganing on

Parnassus" in the sports department; and I think that now another edition of that adolescent volume might be published to catch the not impossible ski trade. At the office I felt merry and elated, for no more tangible reason than sometimes I feel as though all were too difficult for me to cope with. And all day that feeling persisted. And Walter Sinclair writes me about Fred Richardson, who died last week and who once was an artist in Chicago, and drew full-page pictures for the Daily News on Saturdays, for some of which Walter wrote collaborate rhymes, without, he tells me, by-lines, for Mr. Lawson thought that they gave writers exalted notions. "Look," he says, "how George Ade got away after his few by-lines." So all day at the office, working and so home and worked some more, and after a supper of rabbit-stew, early to bed.

Tuesday, January 26

Tiredly up, and to the office, and the news from the laborers and the employers mighty discouraging, and I think this about business: Business like the motor car business is dependent upon the good will of the publick, and if the employers remain callous and obdurate, which rightly or wrongly the publick thinks that they are, and the idea is in the publick mind not because of things that it reads in the Daily Worker but because of what it reads in the capital-owned press, which it seems to me is fair to the labor side, and Lord knows that the newspapers would like to see the strike settled, and to have more motor advertising. So to the dentist's, and thence home and Douglas and Dot Kingston there for supper, and so I later to R. Irvin's, and Gilbert White and Will Tachau there, and we fell to talking of McIntyre and Heath, and Rea was saying that McIntyre said to Heath "Didn't dat train stop?" and we all in concert said what Heath said, which was "Stop? Why, dat train didn't even hesitate." And Gilbert and I fell to talking of Dr. Waite the murderer, for G. knew his wife that was Miss Peck; and her mother and father whom he poisoned. But I recall how I first met him on the tennis court in New Rochelle, on Saturday, June 19, 1915, and I said "A. Waite the chyrurgeon beat me, and badly, but him I found the most chivalrous conqueror of all that have trounced me, no small number, and ever growing, too." And not two years after that he died in the electric chair at Sing Sing, mighty cool and saying that he regretted nothing but the discovery of his crimes.

Tuesday, *February 2*

Lay a long time, with a million maladies surging over me, and so up and to the office, and as I was descending the subway stairs at Twelfth Street I was full of distaste with the world, and especially with the untidyness of the stairs, and a man was ascending, and he was whistling Brahms's First Symphony, that is part of it, and I thought thus shines a good tune in a naughty world. But when I reached the office, the world seemed naughtier than ever, and full of small vanities under the guise of principles, and the throwing away of principles under the guise of the Greater Good. And the world, I thought, is full of fools like me who have the delusion that anything we say or writer can do any good.

Thursday, *February 4*

So read that the meeting of Mr. Lewis and Mr. Knudsen at Detroit again was of no avail, and kept saying "Thrice at the huts of Fontenoy the labour parley failed." But in all the bad news there was one sweetly pleasant bit: that beginning on the First of April the telephone company will no longer charge each month for hand-set telephones, and that will save me one dollar and twenty cents a year, and what I shall do with that money I do not know, but the chances are, based on experience, that I will spend it foolishly. So worked all the morning at my office, and mighty elated to get a set of Edward VIII stamps for my boys from Ed Harden who was my boss on the Chicago Journal in 1904. To play a few games of kelly-pool, and was Fortune's fool, albeit at times I was not unskilful. So home to supper, and heard A. Woollcott tell over the air of two poems that he had read herein, and one was Sarah Cleghorn's, and he said so; and the other was M. F.'s, but he did not say so. So at this and that all evening, discussing matters of litigation, and so to bed.

Tuesday, February 9

This day Mr. George Ade is 71 yrs. of age, which is not old, and tomorrow Will Tilden will be 44 yrs. of age, which is older for a tennis player than 80 is for Mr. Justice Brandeis. Lord! what an elastic thing is age, even in the same person on a single day! For how it is with myself I do not know, but I know that at one time in a day my 10-year-old boy seems like a mature man of forty, and at another time like a baby of two years. Most of the talk I hear is talk against the President, and not only by Republicans and so-called reactionaries, but by Democrats and so-called liberals. None so ill-informed as to have no conviction on the subject, but about the streets cluttered up with motor-cars, which something could be done about, nobody hath time for, such things being too trivial for the millions of master-minds who help make public opinion. Home after work, and in the evening to see "Yes, My Darling Daughter," so adroitly phrased and so felicitously acted by Miss Lucille Watson and Miss Violet Heming and Miss Peggy Conklin, to name but three of them, that I had an evening full of innocent merriment.

Friday, February 12

Up at seven on Lincoln's Birthday, and read the newspapers, and was mighty glad that Mr. Henry Curran the magistrate had decided that there was nought obscene in Jas. Farrell's "A World I Never Made," and he spoke of many four-letter words used in the book, and said that they had been used by great writers since the birth of English literature, and occurred in the works of Shakespeare and Fielding, and he might have added that it was not those words that made Shakespeare Shakespeare nor Fielding Fielding, nor Farrell Farrell. But the American said: "Mr. Farrell was very proud of the decision; Mr. Sumner very dejected." Now "very" is a four-letter word that ought to be ruled out of conversation and writing; and if I were a potent force in the Newspaper Guild I would revise the constitution and make it read that the use of "very" would be just cause to discharge the reporter using it, and the copyreader for not deleting it. So to school, it being Parents' Day, and thence to the office till late afternoon, whence to K. Simpson's, and met there Alf Landon, a gentleman from Topeka; and so in the evening with John G. R. Hunt to the Boston Symphony concert, and so home to bed.

Monday, February 15

Yesterday Dr. Harry Emerson Fosdick, who is a nephew of Harry Castlemon, author of "Frank on a Gunboat," said that the youth of the nation needed religion, and it may be that that is true. Every Monday morning I read what the ministers had said on Sunday, and it generally is that religion is needed. Now I have no quarrel with this, but I do not know another profession in which its professors may do this. I might say that the great need is for more newspaper readers, which also is, if not a truth, at least a debatable point. Now there are those who will say that there are too many newspaper readers already, but I do not mean those who read newspapers and nothing else. But now and then a man tells me that he never reads a newspaper at all, and I do not see how such persons, if they tell the truth about themselves, which they often do not, can live in this sometimes beautiful and oftener sad and aching world.

Sunday, February 21

Early up, and with my boys in the rain to East Millstone, New Jersey, to Peggy Ernst's, they going to see their ponies Gold Leaf and Lucy, in their winter quarters there. So Mrs. Ludwig there, from Nantucket, and fell to discussing the cinema, and we agreed that we had liefer see a second rate play than a first rate cinema. So home by way of Bound Brook, and in the evening with R. Kirby to supper, who tells me that he will fly to Arizona next Saturday for his winter holiday. Then to watch Ralph Greenleaf play Chuck Thomas a game of pool, not much fun, and so played a little myself with H. McGee, much fun, and so home and to bed, and read J. Steinbeck's "Of Mice and Men," liking it mighty much, the best part to me being the hope that the men had for living off "the fatta the lan'," which is a hope that is in all of us and is never realized, for when it is it soon seems like the lean of the land.

Monday, February 22

Two hundred and five years ago this day George Washington was born, which seems like yesterday to some of us. But the country that he was the father of, though an infant as countries go, does not sleep like a baby. And as to the slumber of infants, it is no guess of mine that to sleep like a baby is not always to lie quiet and unlachrymose all night.

And it is far easier to give candy to a child than to take it from him.

Wednesday, February 24

Early to the office, distrait at many things, and at work till nearly five in the afternoon, and then to a party to meet Mrs. Nell Roosevelt, and found her a gracious lady, and she tells me that I have had a salutary effect upon her letters if not upon her life, and I saw Dot Fisher for the first time, too, and she invited me to visit her in Vermont, which I shall do this year or next. So home, and dawdled about all evening, and to bed early.

Saturday, August 6, 1938

Up early but it is because I do sleep neither wisely nor too well, owing to the surcingle I am forced to wear, or zone, or girdle. Yet how smoother any mattress other than hospital mattresses is! Lord! in testaments here and there I have read how one of sound mind bequeathes hospital beds, or a sum of money to a specific hospital. But I beg any about to make such a bequest to make it for a great number of mattresses, the one on my Bed of Pain having been like a corduroy road. And many times I felt like Joe Weber, when he said to Lew Fields, "Meyer, I'm laying on a nail." So all morning read Ruth McKenney's "My Sister Eileen," which I was disappointed in, it being too liberally endowed with hoydenish nostalgia, seeming to me to say, "Weren't we the fascinating little devils?"

Sunday, August 21

Early up, and to an apothecary's for breakfast, it being too early for the coffee to have become stale, and so to meet some persons at 9:30, but they did not arrive for an hour, and I thought, if I could write a novel, I could have written five long ones in the time that I have wasted by my conscientious promptitude. So in the afternoon met C. Fadiman, and indulged in some puerile repartee with him. So home and fell to work with an inventive zest mothered by necessity, until past eleven o'clock, and so mighty weary, to bed.

Monday, *August 29*

To my scrivening betimes, and it occurred to me that the dulness of the Hines trial, some of which is broadcast over the wireless would be enlivened by music, which would be supplied by two singing gentlemen, in solos and duets, the singers being Mr. Thomas Dewey, who studied singing that he might sing in opera, and for aught I know was a member of the Michigan Glee Club; and Mr. Lloyd Stryker, whom I heard sing in "Utopia, Limited," and for aught I know was a member of the Hamilton College Choir, his father having been president of that institution. I had far liefer that they would sing than indulge in puerile repartee. Much talk of Mr. Dewey's becoming a candidate for the Governorship of New York; and I hope, feeling the hope to be futile, that he will emulate General Sherman, who said that if nominated he would not run, and if elected he would not serve. Lord! the water of candour will not mix, it would seem, with the oil of politicks. Yet meseems that Mr. Roosevelt is candid in being militantly interested, or interfering, in state politicks. So, I all the day at work pleasantly enough, the depleting heat being absent. So after dinner to a cinema, to see "Cowboy from Brooklyn," the first time I had been in a place consecrated to entertainment since before I was cut for the stone, and enjoyed it mighty much, and so home and to bed by eleven o'clock.

Thursday, *September 15*

To the office, mighty early, and read all the newspapers about what is happening abroad, and wondered how much of what Hitler said, and what Mr. Chamberlain said, was truth and how much was diplomacy. And how it all should be interpreted. For this I know: The American people are interested mainly in whether, if there be a war in Europe this nation will send troops, as we did 21 years ago. And their second interest is whether there will be war, that is declared war, in Europe. Not that the undeclared wars in Spain and China are not full of horror as any other war. But that England wants peace, as Mr. Chamberlain says, nobody can doubt; I doubt, too, that Hitler is foolish enough to desire war, yet it seems to me that for him to acquire the common sense to want peace would be a sudden piece of lucidity for a man whose mind seems diseased. So heard that Thos. Wolfe had died, and though most of his writings were too verbose for my taste, there was too much greatness in him to die at 37.

Monday, September 19

Early up, and to the city by railroad train, and to my office by subway, in the rain, which falleth on the tennis court and the baseball diamond alike, and so did a vast amount of work and reading the newspapers about the affairs concerning the Czechs, and how Mr. Chamberlain is anathematized, though I am not wise enough to know whether he is the savior of peace or the fomenter of what may be the greatest of wars, and I doubt that many who are mere newspaper readers like myself know much more about it. But Hitler's words, as Catullus hath said of a lady, are writ in running water.

Wednesday, September 21

To the late train with Delia Mullen Newell, she having cared for my children for 11 yrs., and at the Terminal I was too affected to bid her farewell. So in the rain to the office, and Lord! how the rain poured all the morning and the afternoon; so I to the train, but they told me that the trains were not running, and that they might not go past Stamford, and a great crowd milling about, and thronging the telephone booths, and I noticed that men are more garulous than women. So I telephoned, and my wife said that no car could reach the station, the roads being impassable. So I to dinner with R. Irvin, and so D. Wallace and I beat Mr. Houghton and Mr. Richards at a game of pool, and so I to bed. And I bethought that these days some books to read would have been "The Mortal Storm," "The Rains Came," and "The Dark River."

Monday, September 26

Up at six o'clock eastern standard time, but at seven Connecticut time, Governor Cross having decreed another week of late time, that there might be another hour to reclaim some of the utterly depleted places in the State, and I felt that it was good fortune and only that only an elm and an apple tree had been uprooted; so I to the city by train, and to my office, where all day, and in the afternoon heard the voice over the wireless of Adolf Hitler, screamingly hysterical it sounded to me, but perhaps he would consider me merely a whisperer. So there was great talk about it, and some said that it meant war, and some that it meant peace; and President Roosevelt sent an appeal to him, for peace, saying that war would be a horrible thing; and most said that he should have remained mute; but I dissent.

Wednesday, September 28

To the city, and all during the ride I read as much as I could about the matters relative to Czechoslovakia, and it seemed to me that the best that could happen was still a terrible thing, and whilst it was a dramatic thing that I heard this afternoon, how Mr. Neville Chamberlain had told the House of Commons that Herr Hitler had invited him to meet him in Munich the morrow morn, he might have said demanded instead of invited. And that M. Daladier and Sig. Mussolini also had been invited to attend, probably to hear Herr Hitler tell them that he will do whatever they desire him to do, except this and that. That such a person could dictate terms to Great Britain and France seems a humiliating thing, and whilst eternal vigilance is said to be the condition upon which God hath given Liberty to man, the cost of liberty, and of peace, whether temporary or lasting no man cay say, the price that is to be paid for a cessation of threatening bullying will be great. And men will long debate whether it was a brave and wise thing to risk being called a betrayer of Czechoslovakia, in order to muzzle the dogs of war; or whether it was a cowardly thing to compromise with one whose word civilization hath no credence in.

Saturday, October 1

Lay all morning, my throat being so that I could scarcely swallow, and when I did there was no pleasure in it. So read all day the newspapers, and there were great stories of how Mr. Chamberlain and Herr Hitler had come to an agreement that Great Britain and Germany would never fight one another, but there were many semi-subjunctives in the pact, and it seemed to me to be one of those Provided-However-Except contracts, like a lease. And Mr. Chamberlain much excoriated, the articulate portion of the publick, and the newspapers, too, for the most part, saying that he had done an unnecessarily wrong thing; and it seemed to me that this time the majority's opinion is righter than wrong. Yet I know that these are quick judgments, made, some of them, in anger, which distorts that serenity needful for cool verdict.

Tuesday, October 4

Up at seven o'clock and felt well enough to go to the city, and on early train, too, and read how Hitler was likely to take more than he had asked for, or would ask for more than he said that he would be willing to take, and every time something of the sort becomes known, there are many who are astonished, attributing to him the same sort of honor and generosity and love of humanity that they themselves possess. Lord! it seems to me that it is as though a man, duped by gamblers who use marked cards, kept on playing with them, and kept on playing. Or it is not unlike the man who continued to lose at roulette. "Do you not know," said a friend of his, whose name I never knew, "that that wheel is crooked?" "Yes," responded the man. "Then why do you play it?" asked his friend. "Because," said the man, "it is the only wheel in town."

Wednesday, October 19

One of my physicians hearing me cough says, Hey, boy, I will give you something for that. Sold, quoth I. No, he said, some medicine. So I to a true apothecary's whose drugs were quick, and got some eighty-five cent medicine, and so took it, and found it as burning to my throat as so much whiskey. So to the office, and read how Mr. Dewey had been talking at Rochester, and accused the Democratic party, or the New Deal, of corruption in the state and the nation; and I disbelieve these campaign speeches always, for when the campaign is over, the candidates often say that they did not mean what they said in the heat of things; and it is all said to sway voters to their side, which it seldom does. For I believe that if the election were held the day after the candidates are nominated, the result would be the same as on Election Day, after hundreds of thousands of words have been said on platforms. How many Dewey adherents, I wonder, go to a Lehman mass meeting? Or how many Lehman voters to a Dewey? Or are swayed by listening to them on the air, or reading in the newspapers what they say? So left the office early, and took a nap, and in the evening to a book auction in behalf of blind artists, and saw there M. Kennerly, who reminded me of the days when he had a bookshop on 29th Street, and I come in to buy "Once Aboard the Lugger____"

Monday, October 31

This morning to the station, and on the train I was astounded to read how last night the countryside was terrified because of Mr. Orson Welles's radio dramatization of H. G. Wells's "The War of the Worlds," which he wrote more than forty years ago, but Mr. Welles changed Mr. Wells's locale from England to New Jersey, and the traffic lanes were crowded with folk fleeing to the woods, and it was said by the newspapers that some persons were injured, and the town was agog with talk of it, and in the office was much talk of it, and some said that it proved that people were stupid, and that they did not wait to hear or see or even read anything with any thought or care; and some assailed the broadcasters saying that the overdramatization of news or pseudo-news was a menace, but the wild things that are done on the radio for children are in the same vein, and before long children weary of them. And some said it was as if a newspaper carried an eight-column streamer saying that bombs had fallen, and thousands were dead, story on page 10, and on Page 10 it said "Read Our Serial, 'World's End,' beginning tomorrow." But it seemed to me that it was just possible that the newspapers themselves were using a loudspeaker to magnify the importance and calamity of something that seemed to me nothing worse than an actor's mistake. But the silliest thing of all was the thought, expressed here and there, that Mr. Welles did it to advertise himself or the broadcasting system or Mr. Herbert George Wells. So to the country, and at dinner time Harry and Lillian Kaufman come but would not taste our fare, and so in the evening to L. Godowsky's, and he turned on some records, and once he turned on three records of the same piece, one of Chopin's, played successively by three pianists, Horowitz, Godowsky, and Rubenstein, and we were to guess which was which, and I was as good as the musicians in the crowd, albeit I only guessed at it. But I held that it was too technical a matter for me; but Leo agreed with me that a blindfolded audience would not know who was conducting an orchestra unless it was playing something mighty familiar; but most of them would not know then, and as for playing something nobody in the audience had heard there are mighty few who could be certain who was conducting.

Thursday, November 10

At six o'clock up, and it was a mighty chilly morning, the thermometer registering 32 degrees, and there was a fine white frost on the ground, and so to the early train, and to the dentist's, and so to my office. This day the news that cometh from Berlin, of the things that the Nazis are doing to the Jews in Germany, is so cruel as to be incredible in any age; but there is this about Hitler and his followers: that daily it seems that human indecency and savagery can go no further, and daily it seems that yesterday all of us were in error.

Wednesday, January 4, 1939

To breakfast early, and met Jno. Phillips there, and talked of this and that, and of Lincoln Steffens, and he told me of something that had been said of him; that he was a fine and accurate reporter, to set down what had happened and what he had seen, but that his thinking was less noteworthy than his reporting. And I was minded of many who can set down facts, but are poor interpreters of those facts; they are good reporters and bad editorial writers. But one who writes opinions ought to have a veneration for facts and for accuracy. So to the office, and was mighty interested to read President Roosevelt's message to the Congress, and there were many fine things in it, and well said, too. For of what always will be known as the Munich pact he said, "A war which threatened to envelop the world in flames has been averted, but it has become increasingly clear that peace is not assured." So to the terminal to the train, and so home and had an early supper, and thence to the school in Weston, and there were some mighty fine cakes and pasties, and then all the parents played a game, and there were some questions asked about the town, such as why Cobb's Mill was so called, and almost nobody knew that it was the dwelling of Frank Cobb, who made the World's editorial page like nothing before or since.

Wednesday, January 11

To the office, after an inept breakfast at an apothecary's, and mighty weary with having slept in a room that was too warm. All the day there, until time to get an early train, and so fell to a doze, and in the evening I looked at the Roberts "This Side Idolatry," thinking to set Mr. Woollcott by the ears, but Lord! the ears were on the other foot, the author of the book being Carl Eric Bechhofer Roberts.

Monday, January 16

Up early, owing to the necessity of wearing a suit other than what I wore on Saturday, which is the last time I wore one, and it takes a man a long time to change everything from fifteen pockets to fifteen other pockets, whereas when lovely woman stoops to dress-changing, she has no such tedious business to go through, all her paraphernalia being carried in her reticule, and when she changes reticules she pours the contents of one into the other. The snow, especially on the trees, looked mighty handsome as Phoebus 'gan arise. So to the train, not so crowded as in the days of the two-cents-a-mile fare. But in the city streets down-town there was no snow, it having been cleared away; but I doubted that it had been cleared on the properly so-called slum streets of the East Side. There is talk more about the subway looting, and the rumors run between one and a half millions of dollars and one thousand dollars. So all day at work, and so home and read Wm. Faulkner's "The Wild Palms," it being too full of incoherence that seemed to me to be affected and a pose. Yet maybe that is the Faulkner style, and some say that he is great anyway, but I think that lucidity is mighty difficult of achievement, and that it is a great aid to reading, if one object of writing is communication. Lord! when I write a muddy or an obscure sentence, it is because I am indolent or hurried, and I hold those reasons excuses, and spurious. For a writer cannot make a house-to-house canvass, saying, "Please regard my matter leniently, for it was written in a hurry," or "whilst Black Care sat at the horseman's back." Which is to say that "The Wild Palms" is too difficult reading for my taste, and I think that Mr. Faulkner is highly endowed with spinach.

Thursday, February 2

Up early of candlemas, or Groundhog Day, and the legend was that if the aardvark or hedgehog emerges and sees his shadow, there will be six weeks more of winter, which is what might be called an Old Groundhog's tale. Yet I think that there will be six more weeks of winter, and at least six more years of trouble. Now there is a great to-do about the President's secrecy concerning the military defense policy, and Mr. Hiram Johnson, the Senator, says that this country may be eased into war, and never know it. Lord! it assuredly was eased into prohibition and never knew it; and whether it was eased into the world war is a matter of debate, and I think always will be. Many of the liftmen are striking, but it is not so wide a matter of interest as three years ago it was, when almost everybody who dwelt in marble apartments was forced to walk up one or more flights of stairs, and most of the office buildings, including the edifice in which I was then employed. So in the London Observer I saw that Sir Charles Sherrington, past-president of the Royal Society said: "Alcohol has a drugging effect, and so it begins to tamper with the running of the 'machinery,' or 'to monkey the machine,' as in America it would be fittingly termed." Lord! how the British do misuse American figures of speech, for one would monkey with a machine, but meseems that what Sir Charles means is to throw a monkey-wrench into the machinery, which is "deliberately to cause something to go awry," as in Great Britain it would fittingly be termed.

Wednesday, February 22

Betimes up, albeit it was a holiday, being the birthday of, among others, Geo. Washington, who ownd a racehorse named Magnolia, but whose country is now an orphan. To the office, which was busy, despite that the number is 110, Washington Street. The trial of James Hines proceedeth, and whether he be imprisoned or freed from the charges, I make little doubt that the policy, or numbers game will continue, with little abatement, the gambling instinct being too strong to have any punishment weaken. I never have heard anybody speak of racehorses at a track without telling what the odds are or were, and a non-betting horserace is as unthinkable as poker played entirely for fun.

Monday, February 27

Awoke early to find the sweet warm sun shining, so up and to the early train, and all the talk still of Hines, and whether he actually will go to prison, as though there were doubt about it. Which showeth how cynical the people are, and how furmly they feel that it isn't how you play the game but did you win or lose, and how much, and there is some superstition that a political boss is above the law. So to the office betimes and cantered through my stint, and so home upon the 4:32, and to my house before six, the first time I have driven home without even turning on the head-lights, and for the first time I felt that spring was imminent, and I was minded of what Oscar Howard said on the first warm day last April, that it always depressed him, for the first thing you knew it was next winter already.

Sunday, April 9

This morning I began reading John Steinbeck's "The Grapes of Wrath," which is so vital and human and heart-breaking, that to me there was nothing in the book that did not seem utterly true. For here is shown the bravery and basic decency of people who find the terrible swift sword of money and power raised inevitably against them. And it shows, too, the hope that is in men until death, and also that those who have a little will share it far more gladly than those who have much, generosity varying inversely as the square of one's possessions. But Lord! I cannot recall when I have read a better book, or a truer, nor did I try to remember, and I did not put down the book until I had finished it. And I wish that I could have called the whole of the country on the telephone, to say "Read this book." And I say:

From California's Oakland to New York's Rhinebeck,
All should read "The Grapes of Wrath," by John E. Stein-
    beck.

Wednesday, April 19

To work, and finished early but at the office till past four,
so by subway to the train, and met H. Rudkin, who asked
me what I was doing in the vicinage of Wall Street, and I
said that there my office is, and he said that he thought
newspaper offices were on 42nd Street, and that many
attorneys had moved thereabout, but I said that I could not
afford to move the presses, etc., just to be near the train;
and he tells me, he hath been driving through South Carolina,
and along the back roads, to see how things were, and he
said that the negroes seemed working and prosperous, and
that in the cotton-fields they got $5 a week, and some about
$2.50; and I said that I did not consider that anything even
if it kept on the 52 weeks a year, which I am certain that it
does not, but that poverty and its handmaid ill health are
widespread; and I told him to read John Steinbeck's "The
Grapes of Wrath," and he said "What does he call it?" and
I said "The Grapes of Wrath," and so do I, for that is its
title. But it is a book that I feel sure that he would mislike.

Sunday, April 23

Early up, and at work, and I felt indignation at Mr. Taft,
the Ohio Senator, who accused Mr. Roosevelt of making a
great to-do about matters in Europe, as though they might
not become of vital importance to us, and neglecting matters
at home, which were vital. And his implication was that all
this was done to draw attention away from domestic troubles.
Which is nonsense, but dangerous nonsense. Yet I am in
favour of criticising the President, and if a man of Mr.
Taft's prominence said such things in Germany about Herr

Hitler, he would not live to repeat such things. And if a man suspected of Communism said them, he would be reviled in what is called the press. To call the newspapers the press is metonomy. So in the afternoon I fell to reading C. S. Forester's "Captain Horatio Hornblower," a tale of frigates and brigs, and fighting mariners, and I could not lay the book down for fascination of the story and the unpretentious stuff about ships, and fell to wondering why I could read Forester and could not read Conrad, who always has seemed pretentious to me, and a little spurious. But the only weak part of the book was toward the end, when dreams come true, albeit I felt that he would be bored soon, and that Mr. Forester would not let him vanish.

Monday, May 15

Betimes up, and to the office, and read how Mussolini yesterday hath said that there were not at present in Europe problems big enough or acute enough to justify a war, which many thought to mean that he said that war was needless, but "at present" gives him what the street urchins would call an out, for he might well say that "at present" means Sunday, May 14, 1939, but not Monday, May 15. Also that whilst Italy desired no war, it might be forced into it by the United States. For nowhere did any warring nation or fraction thereof fight whose quarrel was not just. Sing booh! to them; pooh! pooh! to them. And that's what I should say. All day at the office, and in the evening to the cinema theatre, to see "Good Bye, Mr. Chips," which amazed me with the bright and unobtrusive excellence of its acting, and as for the film being so British that such a teacher is not credible in this nation of so-called utilitarianism, that is nonsense. For even I have known men not dissimilar to Mr. Chips, and have at least three as teachers, Victor Alderson, Thomas C. Roney, and Henry Saunders; and I would guess that many a Yale boy has felt thus about Will Phelps; and Wilbur Cross, who might well be the hero of a film called "Uncle Toby."

Monday, June 12

Read this morning of the visit of King George VI and Queen Elizabeth to Hyde Park, and it all seemed merry enough, yet it may well have been a strain on both pairs, the monarchical and the democratic. And when there has been sung "God Save the King," which we know as "America," which is the German song "Heil Dir im Siegerkranz." And yesterday, as the King and the Queen left Hyde Park, hundreds of the citizenry sang "For He's a Jolly Good Fellow," which is nothing at all but the French song, "Malbrouck s'en va-t-en guerre." But I wondered what was meant by Dr. George Moor, who said in a sermon yesterday, "This land was preserved for the Anglo-Saxon race by the providence of God." Now I am a godly man, and I do not believe that God or his providence ever had the Anglo-Saxon race in mind when He preserved this land. And what would Dr. Moor think if Hitler, or a Hitler-dominated minister said that "Germany was preserved for the Aryan race by the providence of God." For whilst the Great Jehovah may have assisted in the founding and preservation of this land, the principal agent was the Continental Congress, as canny a lot of fellows as ever got together. So finished my work with dispatch, and so home by early train, and for a preprandial immersion in the Copper cool pool, a phrase I liefer would write than speak.

Monday, July 24

Up, and to the city early, and wondered why the great mass of the people will not attend the World's Fair, and I wonder whether it can be widespread unemployment, though I know that the per capita wealth is greater than in 1893, when the people thronged to Chicago, and not by automobile, either. Oh, dear, what can the matter be, Johnny won't visit the Fair. Great Britain, I read, hath recognized the special rights of the Japanese Army in China, which Mr. Chamberlain says is no change in her policy in China. There is talk that the state of business is improving, and many companies are earning much more than they did last year, yet the attitude of some of these business men that hate Mr. Roosevelt seems to be, "Business is good, and gosh! how I dread it!" Mrs. Roosevelt wrote about the so-called bread-and-butter letter sent by the Royal Pair, but not that the King said, as he slid down the banisters, "I do like a little bit of butter for my bread!" To the country, and for a swim in the pool, and at Cooper's for dinner, and R. Hart and Mrs. H there, too, and then there were shewn color-motion pictures of the 4th of July tennis tourney, and I seemed mighty agile, yet some thought that it was slow-motion film, especially of my service. So home before eleven, and to bed.

Wednesday, August 30

Betimes up, and read the newspapers with more tenseness than I have been doing for a month, feeling that I must not omit anything, lest there be something that I had passionate convictions about. Soto my rural atelier, the I'm Alone, and fell to writing, and found it far from irksome, and was at it until the late afternoon, and so the post office, and read in the evening papers that matters in Europe seem awry. Yet I feel that if democracy is not healthy enough to continue where it now prevails, the people in those lands do not deserve it. Lord! those of us who never have known aught but freedom find it hard to conceive what restrictions are, let alone life under despotism. So to supper, and thenafter read to my boy a few chapters of "Great Expectations," some of it better than I had remembered, for when I was a lad and read books I glanced through to see whether there was a lot of dialogue as opposed to "description," which I did not like, but now I find better than most dialogue.

Saturday, September 2

Last night I was apprised that the vespertime journals would be issued on Monday, Labour Day, the first time in many years, albeit in the days before 1912 they were issued on every holiday, even on the Fourth of July, Christmas, and New Year's. So I up early and to the city, to my office, and wrote a few words, and so home again, and on the train I read Hitler's "Mein Kampf," which seemed to me to be the work of a paranoiac, and a verbose one, at that. So to Frances Harrington's for dinner, and Mr. and Mrs. H. Nolde from Reading in Pennsylvania there, and B. Darnton, and some talk of politics, and of labor conditions in the north and the south, and matters grew tense, so we all fell to talking of the chances of war, and some thought that there would be no war, and some that if there were a war it would end in two months, but I fear that there will be a war and a long war, and that at the end of it the warring nations, and even the non-warring nations will be no better off than they are today.

Sunday, September 3

Very early up, and heard that England had declared war against Germany, and now I know that the same lies will be told us by nations at war, and that their slightest victories will be stressed and their greatest defeats minimized. It sickens me to think of who will bear the great burden of the war, and how many million innocent and peace-loving men, women, and children will suffer death and disease. So played some tennis in the afternoon, without much heart to it, and so home and heard President Roosevelt speak upon the war, and how his administration would do its utmost to keep the nation physically neutral.

Thursday, September 7

To the early train, and to the office betimes, and finished my stint to get home in good season, and Paul and Clire Sifton and their two boys there, and all had dinner, and thenafter the boys to bed, and we all sat about and heard many things about matters in Washington, and how many there to think that Mr. Roosevelt will have the Democratic nomination again, there being not anybody else who might win.

Friday, September 8

On the train I read a piece in the Nation of Kenneth Crawford's, from Washington, and the first paragraph answered many things that all are asking:

> The European crisis has pulled enough foliage off the Washington trees to give a clear view of the woods. Frankness induced by tension has cleared up several important questions. For example: Is the Roosevelt Administration neutral? Certainly not. Is there any chance for the United States to stay out of another world war? Practically none. Will the Roosevelt program of liberal reform go on in the event of a general war? It will not. Would such a war solve the country's more pressing economic problems? Temporarily, yes. Would the outbreak of war mean a third term for President Roosevelt? Probably.

At the office until late, and so home, mighty weary.

Sunday, September 10

Gazing from my window this morning, I thought it must be too early to rise, so slumbered again and it was ten when I awoke, still dark and showery. So I up, and put in the morning reading the newspapers, and feeling no elation at the state of things, the whole matter being, as Gilbert hath it, a pretty mess, and a how-de-do. So all the morning at work. Lord! I am low-spirited that nobody in the world wants war, to hear their hypocritical statements, yet many millions of persons are engaged in it, to the exclusion of all other interests and desires. War, say they all, was forced upon us. To me it seems that those who detest President Roosevelt say that he is driving us into war, for his own political ends, and those who believe in his honesty say that he is doing, and will do his utmost to keep us from active participation, in the latter group of which I am. So dawdled about the house all afternoon till supper, and we had calves' brains and eggs, somebody having told my wife of my distaste for the monotony of the Sunday supper. Worked this evening with Timmy on percentage, and he being interested in baseball, he made progress about batting averages, though when I said "If a player had 100 times at bat and got 80 hits, what would his average be?" he said, and properly, "Boy! who was he?"

Tuesday, September 19

Early up, and to the office, where all day, all the talk in and out of the newspapers being about the war, and all hoping that Germany would lose, yet I do get anonymous letters telling me not to say anything against Germany. So to dinner with Jack Moses, and so out, and met a young woman who was Retta Shroder in 1899, and I had not seen her since, and was delighted to talk with her. And I met

Mr. Coggeshall, who tells me that he was the embarcation officer that put me aboard the Leviathan in March, 1918, which brought back vividly the war, and the ineffable boredom of it. Yet my greatest fear is that many things will be said to those, who in a war more than twenty years ago. Such as "This is different," and "That was a long time ago, and you are old that once were young," and "Why did you go in that war if you don't believe in war?" But if this nation, Heaven forbid, should become involved as a combatant, there will be even easier recruiting, I fear, than there was in 1917. For there are more millions of unemployed to whom even a private's pay, with food and lodging furnished, would be a step up. And always there are millions whose life at home is such that they think that any change would be an improvement.

Saturday, September 30

Lay long on a murky morning, and so up, and I hear that the parodic song ending "What's the use of Goering? He never was worth while. So pack up your Goebbels in your old kit bag, and Heil! Heil! Heil!" was written by Sir John Squire, which is nothing to be astonished at forasmuch as nobody, to my notion, ever write such superb parodies as Jack Squire, they being, I think, worth more than the rest of his so-called serious verse. And it made me think that there is something nowadays like a guilty feeling about many writing persons who think that unless they write about cosmic affairs they should give themselves up to the constabulary, and that they will be so many Neros fiddling while Rome is burning. But I think that if a man be a professional violinist, he serves the world better by fiddling than by being a member of a volunteer fire department.

Friday, October 6

To the office, tired with unrest last night, and read of Hitler's talk, it being the same old "I was fair with England, but my patience has been strained." So home early, to take care of the house, everybody else but Puff and Jack being away from it.

Wednesday, October 11

Up, at ten in the morning, and so had a great breakfast of some citrus fruit and ham and eggs and some toast and coffee, and so to the office and did my work with great gusto, and so to the train, and when I emerged found my wife on it, who tried to make me guess whom she had luncheon with, and I could not, so she told me that it was Sinclair Lewis, and that he was so engrossing that it was half past three when she left. So home to supper, and heard Mr. Fred Allen's comicalities on the air, till Tim came downstairs and said, Papa, don't laugh so; I can't sleep.

Monday, October 16

Mighty early up, and out to see whether it was as cold last night as I thought it was, and it was, for the flowers were all black, as though they were in mourning for the summer. So to the city, and on the way to my office I wondered why motorists are the most illiterate class of all, forasmuch as it seems that they cannot even read a sign that says No Parking in This Block. So at this and that detail of my profession of fitting type to a space and proof-reading, and so to dinner with Mrs. Pauline Fadiman and her husband and my wife, and so to see "The Man Who Came to Dinner," mighty comic, and as bitter a satire as ever I saw, and superbly acted, too, and Mr. M. Wooley, who acted the part of Alexander Woollcott, did it elegantly and ribaldly, saying many things that the Town Sobber might have said, and in truth, many things that he has said. So thenafter to have some brown October gingerale, and all fell to talking, and my wife said that I had no sensation, but that I had intuition, and what that means I have not enough intuition to know, but I experienced the sensation of listening to nonsense, which I said, but she either had the sensation of deafness or the courtesy to ignore my criticism. So to bed, thinking of that book called "It Is Later Than You Think."

Wednesday, November 8

Lay a long time this morning, having lain awake cursing the noise made by the power house on 19th Street, which I doubt is a necessary noise. So read the papers about yesterday's election, and so had a fine breakfast of ham and eggs. To the office, and in the afternoon went uptown to have a nap, and in the evening with my wife to dinner, and thence to the Empire, to see "Life With Father," which I enjoyed mighty much, Mr. Lindsay and Miss Stickney being flawless. They enacted Mr. and Mrs. Clarence Day, as he stormed about a good deal, and my wife nudged me and said "Just like you," which so angered me with the injustice of it that had I had an aisle seat I should have flounced out from the place. It was mighty true to life when Mrs. Day indulged in money transactions that were extravagant and fantastic, and put me in mind of matters in my own home, such as sending dresses to the gentleman who irons my suits for 69¢, the dresses costing $5.25 to repair and press.

Sunday, November 19

So read the newspapers, and saw that young Beach Conger of the Herald Tribune had been thrown out of

Germany for hinting things unfavorable to Hitler. Lord! what a country we live in, and how thankful we should be that anybody may hint or print things unfavorable to the President, and the columns printed in disfavour of altering the tradition of the Thanksgiving date would fill ten shelves in the Roosevelt Library which was dedicated this day, the anniversary of the Gettysburg Address. So all day at home, save for calling for the Hall boys and Austin Stevens and my boys at the cinema palace, and driving them home. Great talk about double Thanksgivings, and we sang "Thanksgiving comes but twice a year in this part of this hemisphere." To bed by nine o'clock.

Sunday, November 26

Up, and to the village for the newspapers, and read them all the morning and did a little work, too, and then took my boy Jack for a ride in the country, up Fanton Hill. And so home to dinner, and after it worked until I fell asleep. So in the late afternoon to Wm. Wisner's, and had a merry time of it for the most part, albeit I did not like that a young man from Wilton, Mr. E. Everett Smith, Jr., whom I never had met, said to me that he could not read the miserable sheet I worked for, and I told him that owing to the Bill of Rights a man no longer could be put into jail for failing to read any paper; but how he could dislike it without reading it I forgot to ask. But he asked me about Mr. Kernan and Mr. Faydiman, and I wonder whether he thinks journalism is an accurate science. But his wife Elise told me that she dreamed of me, which may be why he would not read my Miserable Sheet. But I had a pleasant time with Ann Arnold, and many others, and so home and to bed after supper, a little after eight o'clock.

Monday, December 18

To the city by the early train, and heard that Heywood Broun had died whilst I was on the way to the office, and it was a mighty great loss to bear, albeit there were many of us who marveled more than ten years ago that he kept on living, with the poor care that he took of his person, and yet I doubt that there are any other persons in this nation that so have captured the affections of the reading public as he. And I thought, for many have commented on his recent conversion to the Roman Catholic Church, how religion had played a great part not only in his writings but in his frivolous conversation. And I was minded how often, in card games he would curse his ill-luck, and then, fearing lest it continue, he would say, looking upward, "Forgive me, God; I was only kidding." And I am convinced also that if Mr. Ralph Pulitzer and Mr. Roy Howard never had interfered with him, or antagonized him, the rebelliousness that caused him to be discharged would have been less conspicuous, but no less vigorous. For I know well that many of the things that his publishers objected to were done to prove to himself that he was the wearer of no man's collar, and Heaven knoweth frequently not of his own. But it is hard to write of a man so polygonal and polyhedral. But whilst it is true that he had a deep love for humanity, I doubt that he liked anybody so enormously well as to have what the rest of us might call close or enduring friendships. Perhaps he thought that such things hampered him. But I knew that many of the eulogists would say that there was no malice or bitterness in him, and that is not true. And I made a search for something I once said about Finley Peter Dunne, and it is equally true of Broun. Thus: "For editors, fearful of calling names, feel that the advertisers and the politicians and the social leaders—money, politics, and social

ambition being the Achilles heels of editors and publishers—
are journalisms's sacred cows. But if pretense and hypocrisy
are attacked by the office clown . . . the crooks and the
shammers think that it is All in Fun. And when the Dunnes
and the Lardners die, the papers print editorials saying that
there was no malice in their writing and no bitterness in
their humor. Few popular writers ever wrote more mali-
ciously than Lardner and Dunne. They resented injustice,
they loathed sham, and they hated the selfish stupidity that
went with them." And I would add Broun's name to that
pair.

Sunday, December 31

Up mighty early, and cast up accounts of the year, and
I was dejected at the state of the world, yet knew that it
had emerged from even worse oppression and apparent
insanity many times before now. As to the nation, it is in
comparatively a happy condition, yet I think that we are
likely to become complacent about our freedom and our
democracy. For freedom must continually be fought for,
and as the song hath it, it is something that hath a battle-
cry. Save for a cough, I am well; and less in debt than last
year I was, for which I thank Heaven. And my budget for
1940 is lower than it was for the year closing. My work hath
more often dissatisfied me than not, and I resolve to have
those days of unworthy work fewer, which I can do by taking
more thought to it, and not being diverted by material
matters and tiny irritations. So at noon to the train, and
met P. Wing at the station, and on the train we to the buffet
car, and I had some ham and eggs. So to meet some friends,
and the subject arose of the date of Lincoln's Gettysburg
Address, which occurred on November 19, which is Anthony's birthday. But Jas. A. Garfield also was born on that
date, and Jos. Di Maggio was married last Nov. 19. So

waited about for the 7 o'clock train, P. Wing having promised to be thereon and drive me home, but he was not so I must needs hire a car, for $2.50.

Tuesday, January 9, 1940

This morning I read all of Mr. F. Roosevelt's speech at the dinner given to commemorate the Battle of New Orleans, and it seemed to me mighty good humored, but when the President said that being President had been fun, I felt that certain persons who blame him for all their woes, some of which are traceable to their own indolence and selfishness, will say that he is the only one who has had any fun in eight years, and similar balderdash. Lord! when I read the bill of fare, and learned what they had for dinner, I felt hungry, albeit I was less than one hour from having had a giant breakfast. At the office a long time, working against my desire to stay from the office utterly on the morrow morn. So to dinner, and thence uptown, and saw Miss Ferber, and her nieces, Janet and Minna, who often, I make no doubt, are called the Little Foxes. Thence to play at cards, and I had great good fortune, but not the wisdom to run away, and little by little it was Good Bye, the Messrs. Chips. So to bed.

Monday, February 19

Today was published the Republican Program Committee's report outlining a course for adoption at the convention, which said, in many words that the government should Let Business Alone, which is the same wail that some of the Democrats and what he called the Malefactors of Great Wealth said about the Republican Theodore Roosevelt. Yet the songs, that all American of all parties could unite in singing would be Hail Columbia, comparatively happy land! and Shouting the Battle Cry of More Freedom than You Can Whisper Anywhere Else. Lord! it seems to me that there is so much propaganda of one kind and another that I should not be astounded if some children would refuse to decline *mensa* unless they could be assured that it was a union made table. Also I thought of Tommy Dewey, and what can he know of England and Finland and Russia and Italy and Germany and foreign affairs and thought that only a small part of the United States knows? Mr. Dewey strikes me as a humorless fellow, and while most famous men also are humorless, like Mr. Hitler, such men, I think are without sympathy with their fellow men. Some say that it is a mistake to see both sides, but I do not agree. Often the man who sees only one side gets a reputation for Devotion to a Cause, as well as sincerity. And the man who can see both sides gets a reputation for being wishy-washy. I do not agree with that. On an early train home.

Saturday, March 16

Lay long this morning, and so met Tim on the train, and drove him home, there being a light snow, and then at once to the station to meet my daughter Puffy, and in those few minutes the snow was deep, and whilst driving I began a set of verses,

> I am weary of the winter;
>> It is more than I can stand,
> Especially in the hinter-
>> Land.

> I am far from being petty
>> On the city winter; but
> I am sick of snow in old Connecti-
>> Cut.

but I could not finish them. So worked a little in the afternoon, the trombone player having gone to Fairfield to practice. So to bed early in the evening, and waked many times in the night by the noise of some one gently tapping, and I muttered that it must be some rodent visitor, but after much investigation found that it was the flapping of a placard on a door, reading "Do Not Disturb."

Monday, March 25

Of yesterday it might have been said "No chill upon an Easter day is half so sad a blight," for the first time in my memory the pipes congealed. Much talk about two Republican candidates for the nomination, Mr. Dewey and Mr. Vanderberg, and I gathered that Mr. Vandenberg does not have any affection for Mr. Dewey, though it may be that next summer one of them will make speeches in behalf of the other, albeit both of them may have to mount the rostrum, as they say in the National capital, in behalf of Wendell Wilkie, who seemeth to me the most forthright of the Republicans. Politics and war the newspapers are replete with, and stories of crime, and of Russell-baiting, but of matters that might make the city a pleasanter place to live, such as a lessening of subway crowding, and a considerable alleviation of the habit of keeping motor-cars on the street for many hours at a time, they do nought about. Lord! I would put war matters on page 2, and politics, until convention time, on page 3. I wish that I became less indignant about matters of journalism, and could feel that it all is unimportant, instead of feeling that it is the weightiest thing of all. Home by early train, in the daylight.

Sunday, April 7

With my boy Anthony to Fairfield, to have a look at the Unquowa School, and so home and walked about in the warm sunshine, and so indoors, and read a mystery tale,

"The Wedding Guest Sat on a Stone," and I could not choose but skip. Fell to thinking about matters abroad, which are in no good way, and lashed myself into a fury growing angry at persons who continue to ask what I know about the war, as though anybody connected with journalism had access to things that nobody else had, and as though if anybody like that knew anything it would not be printed with all possible haste. So now I tell them that Germany is about to throw Stalin over, and sign a non-aggression pact with Great Britain, which is all right, save that they then begin to argue. And I know only what I read in the newspapers, and seldom do I read all the war news even in them. It hath been said that Tommy Dewey is a man who hath no lighter or humorous side, which is a great asset for one who wants to be a dominator, and I wondered whether Hitler ever had laughed at anything, and if so at what, and how long ago it was.

Monday, May 13

Betimes up, and early to the city, reading the news of the imminent Nazi occupation of Holland, and it kept running through my head a book of Henty's, "By Pike and Dyke," only what it was about I do not recall; nor much of Reade's "The Cloister and the Hearth," save that it concerned Erasmus. Yet how sad the news must be to my Dutch friends, Hendrik Van Loon and Eugen Boissevain, I can not imagine, for this country is too large for most of us to feel that way, and I thought that we here could feel that way only about towns, talk as we will about the great nation. For I conjecture that I should feel far worse about the fall of Chicago than about the fall of Arizona. To the country early, and tried to read, but could not keep my mind on aught but the war, and the feeling that would not down that I have two boys who already are paying full fare on the railroads.

Wednesday, May 15

Up at about ten o'clock, and made no haste to attain to the lower part of the city, and still the news from Europe causes reason to totter. Mr. Churchill the new British Prime Minister gives no rosy picture of the future. Some of the military students, or experts, as some call them, make a parallel between this and the war of 1914–18, in that for three and one half years the Germans, save for minor conflicts, seemed victorious. But this time, the Germans are better prepared and the enemies of Germany worse prepared. So by early train home, and to sleep before ten, lulled by the susurrus of the radio.

Sunday, May 19

All the news this morning is bad, and among such things is the merely partisan hitting out at the President, which, like him or not, is as futile as hitting out at the weather, foasmuch as the President is the only one we have, and the weather, such as it is at any time, is the only weather we have. It brings to mind those who were wont to keep the windows closed at night, because of the night air, yet at night that is all the air that there is. Heard in the afternoon Mr. Winston Churchill on the wireless, nor was there any false optimism in his talk.

Monday, June 17

Up, and full of a zestful feeling, and so to the train, and read the papers, and five minutes later I felt weary and ill, having read the dread news from France, and the feeling that the morrow's would be worse, and so on, and wondering whether murder and cruelty reach a saturation point, or grow greater with each fresh crime. And yet, alas, there was nothing secret about the great preparation that Germany was making all these years. But I greatly resent the many utterances that the democracies had grown soft with love of ease and comfort, for, whilst a slave race may starve and deprive itself of material things, it will not do so unless scourged and beaten into submission. For I do not believe that most of the human race, even the Germans, want to do the minimum amount of work for the maximum pay.

Tuesday, June 18

Early up, to gather roses while I may, and so with R. Irvin to the town, and we noted that nobody near us was reading the sport news, or anything but war news and leader-pages. And at the office there was an air of soberness. Great interest in the first issue of the new newspaper, called PM, nor could I find any who did not say "I am disappointed," but I thought that it was the best first number of a new publication in my time, which means the Daily News and the New Yorker. And I think that its mistakes are rectifiable, and that it takes much time for momentum to gather. And once gathered it takes time to stop.

Saturday, July 13

Very early up, to the village to get the newspapers, and more and more is the talk of politics whether Mr. Roosevelt is to stand again for re-election, and it seems to me that all the ideas about going counter to tradition are silly, for they say that G. Washington had no third term, yet it was only because he was too ill to take it. And as to the tradition set by Jefferson and Jackson, it is going against that tradition to travel by train or airplane, and to use electric light. Mr. Coolidge and Mr. Hoover went against tradition in even listening to the radio. And the aspect of the world did not change in a week's time in the spacious days of Jefferson and Jackson, so a fig, which is a traditional fruit, say I, for tradition if tradition stand in the way of progress! So to the court for most of the day, and so home and found S. and Marion Chase come for lodging whilst their house is undwellable for the nonce, or even longer.

Tuesday, September 17

Yesterday my aged son of 13 yrs. had his first day in a school in Fairfield, and he tells me that it is a fine school, and I asked him in what regard, and he said they had lamb and mashed potatoes and gravy for lunch. So up and to the city by train, and still the news, censored though it is, is of death and destruction, and among the things destroyed forever is any romance about being a war correspondent, for there is no longer a front, or first lines to be behind. Lord! seven weeks from this day we shall vote for Electors, and if Connecticut's 8 votes are cast for Mr. Roosevelt, I shall win a tidy sum from K. Simpson, for

> From Stonington to Greenwich,
> From Salisbury to Lyme,
> From Staffordsville to Saugatuck,
> It's Roosevelt every time.

Thursday, September 19

I do envy those persons who, commenting upon the war, are certain of why Germany or England or France does this, or has done that, I being mighty much confused by what is going on in the world. When I consider how my light is spent, in reading what is available to all who have two cents, and still I am unable to know, how is it, I wonder that the gentlemen I hear upon the train, or upon the subway, know so many things? And I have noticed that when there are two men, one of them talks continuously and the other either listens or lets his thoughts wander elsewhere. Mr. Willkie,

I read, says it is true that the President has lost faith in us, meaning the people. And I say that it is untrue. I have no faith in 130,000,000 people to decide matters for themselves beyond choosing a President, nor do I think that Mr. Willkie has faith in the American people to do certain things, and less faith in the TVA than in the C. & S. Lost my temper this afternoon, like a fool, over irksomeness at telephoning. But home in good spirits, and to bed by ten o'clock.

Thursday, September 26

At work from early morning until late afternoon, and so home, and met Jas. Kieran on the train, and talked of this and that, of craftsmanship in journalism and politics, and I home to supper, and so did some work until ten o'clock and so to bed, but lay and listened to W. Willkie make a speech in Omaha, and after the first applause died, said: "You touch Mrs. Willkie and I very much," and I could hardly believe my ears that a university graduate whose wife was a librarian could use such English, and it ill becomes one who uses such grammar to get out his hammer and scorn what he called the accent of Groton, Harvard, and Hyde Park, which even the Roosevelt-haters must admit is clear and articulate. Now I do not imply that a grammarian would make a good president, nor that one who misspeaks the language would be bad; but the odds are in favor of one who observes what he reads, albeit Mr. Willkie may have been reading Ring Lardner this afternoon.

Thursday, October 17

Up, and found that the night wind had blown down so many leaves that I did a deal of raking early in the morning, and still the place looked like East Vallambrosa Junction. So to the station unhurried, and in the train met with R. Irvin, the Newtown Pippin, and talked about what little

fuss there seemed to have been made about the draft registration, and to say sooth, I think there would have been
not much more if it had been a registration for a draft to
send men actually to fight, instead of preparation to resist
possible invasion. Now I think also that not only young men
but also older men, and most women, care less about the
democracy that they hear about, and which having do not
value much, but would greatly price if deprived of, than
they care about their hatred of Hitler and Hitlerism. For one
who lives in a democracy, and who always has lived in one,
thinks no more about it than a man in perfect and continuous
health does about his health. To the Automobile Show, and
I thought all these new cars were mighty good to see, and
shinier than any car I have had since 1925. So to the office,
and by the end of the afternoon home, and in the evening
began reading "The Fire and the Wood," good as far as I
read, 100 pp., and so fell asleep.

Monday, October 28

On Saturday afternoons throughout this pleasant and
peaceful land, which I feel it always will be, the ball is passed
on hundreds of gridirons. But the rest of the time these
lovely autumn days and nights the lie is passed on hundreds
of rostrums, and over dozens of microphones. And these
orators, on both sides, shy away from issues, and vent their
malice and scorn on persons instead of things, such as a true
unity among the states and their people. And it seems to me
that it is silly for Mr. Willkie to imply that the nation will
be of no account unless he is President. And I have seen no
mention of whether his ally, Jno. Lewis, will cause him to
make all employes of the corporation he was the head of
join the Congress of Industrial Organizations. To work early,
and finished by 2 in the afternoon, and so home, and in the
evening listened to the President make a fine speech, the only

flaw being that he termed Martin, Barton, and Fish alliteration; when alliteration would be Bitten, Batten, Barton, and Burton.

Tuesday, November 5

Very early up, and to the Town Hall before breakfast, and so voted, and in less time than it taketh to tell it, a cross shewing where the good deed was committed. So home, and found that Tim had missed the school bus, so I drove him to school, and so home to breakfast, and made me ready to go the city, where I did not arrive until one in the afternoon, and finished work, with MacKinlay Kantor's help, in an hour, and so uptown for a short nap, and a game of pocket billiards, and so uptown to Radio City, to hear how the election might be going, and before eight o'clock it was certain that Connecticut had voted Democratic, albeit the Town of Weston voted Republican in all possible ways, and voted 440 for Willkie, and 234 for Roosevelt. And in 1936 it voted 283 for Landon and 213 for Roosevelt. So met Mr. Hanson, a Compo Beach boy, and he told me where were some sandwiches, of which I consumed many. So to a meeting to say goodby to Bill King and some others, and so hastened to the station, but stopped long enough to have some ginger-ale, and to the train to Poughkeepsie, and thence to Hyde Park, where were some gathered to hear the verdict of the people, and it was near midnight when I got there, and it seemed certain that the majority of the popular vote as well as that of the College of Electors had chosen Mr. Roosevelt, which I and others there were happy about. Yet albeit my feet were jubilant, the rest of me felt that the nation was beginning a new era, rather than that the election had been decided. And I felt that the victory was more impressive, though less in actual magnitude, than four years ago. And so all out on the porch, and the President talked to a great crowd from the village that had come to wish him well, and he spoke with great felicity. So to say good night to him, and I felt a great solemnity about it all, and deeply grateful to live in a nation that had chosen so happy a warrior, whose heart is as stout as it can be merry, but whose soul is good and whose mind is tough. So to an inn at Poughkeepsie, at past three in the morning, and to bed.

Wednesday, November 13

A warm and drizzling morning, and learning that the Athenians are not only resisting the Romans, but attacking them. And I was minded to play with "Then up spake Mussolini, A leader loud was he, Now who will stand at my right hand, And bomb the Greeks for me?" But in his army may be many false Sextii.

Thursday, November 14

Up, and to breakfast with L. Bemmelmanns, and so out in a rainy morning, without benefit of umbrella, and to my office, where the news from Taranto is as excellent as any news of war may be, which is that the British Royal Air Force had worked great havoc upon the Italian Navy, and that means not only that the ships were lost, but also many men must have been killed. This day I hear that the Social Science book by Harold Rugg has been forbidden by the Board of Education in Mount Vernon, and that the American Legion thought that they did not promote what it called true Americanism. I have just bought six of the junior high school Rugg books for my son, and I have read them, and I was delighted with the broad common sense of them, and thought how far that kind of textbook had advanced since we had to learn things from Barnes's "History of the United States," in which this nation was the hero of an Algeresque story, and the English all were bad, and the

Revolutionists all wonderful. So took R. Harrington home in my petrol-waggon, and so to supper and to bed at eight o'clock.

Saturday, December 7

This day a sadness overcame me, forasmuch as a year ago this day Heywood Broun called me and bade me come to his house to celebrate his birthday, but I could not go out, I being abed, and having taken medicine to ward off pneumonia. So all day at home, and read in Owen Wister's "Roosevelt: The Story of a Friendship," though to me it seemed more like idolatry. Not that I thought that phase unwelcome, after all the deflationary biographies there are. But I got a far better idea of Theodore Roosevelt, and the things within himself that must have torn his spirit, and what seemed to me the compromises he had made with his conscience. And perhaps that interested me so greatly because in my life I have made compromises with my conscience, and postponed the doing of unpleasant tasks, and even have delayed thinking, using the hypnosis of games or of reading to postpone work.

Wednesday, December 25

Early this morning, Jack and Puffy and Tim come in my bed, ostensibly to wish me a happy Christmas, albeit I had liefer rest merry. But I took it with a good grace, and so we all up to look at the stockings hung by the chimney with mighty little care, and all overjoyed at the gifts. So all the morning in innocent merriment, including the playing of many Alec Templeton records, Tim's present. So to dinner, good, and big; and in the afternoon to the city by train, and met my boys and Arthur Otis and 3 Siftons, and we all to hearken to Mr. Frederick Allen, mighty amusing to me, albeit Anthony laughed so loud I missed some of the allenol tablets, as some wit has called them. So my boys and I to an inn, and forthwith to bed.

Tuesday, January 7, 1941

Up, and with K. Simpson, the Gentleman from New York, to the Library of Congress, and had a talk with A. MacLeish, and so to meet Mr. Wagner the Senator, and mighty much impressed with him, and much taken with the unpretentiousness of him, and also how well-garbed he is. So to the White House, where the President talked to the journalists, and I thought that he seemed a little weary albeit marveled at his patience and lack of irritation, when in his place I should have screamed. So in the evening Albert Warner caught me up, and so home with him to dinner, and later D. Richberg come in, and I told him the last time I had seen him he was a mile-walker at the University of Chicago, and he showed me how he did it, and mighty alactritous, he being in the Class of 1901. So home, and all professing to disbelieve that it was midnight, which it was.

Wednesday, January 8

Up, and did some work, and so to J. Alsop's for luncheon, and found Mrs. Alice Longworth there, and all mighty pleasant for me, they two conversing in fine style, and we all looked at a book of Roman sculpture, and they found resemblances in politics to all the pictures, but I did not know most of the names of the people named. So all afternoon at work, and at six to J. Forrestal's and stopped an hour, and thence to dinner alone, and when I was finished Chas. Wilson come to sit with me, and tells me he is from Peoria, and we talked of Geo. Fitch, who was on the Herald Transcript with him. So early to bed.

Monday, January 20

Early up, and to the office, and read about the great crowds in Washington to see the Inauguration, and to hear the first Third Inaugural Address of the nation. So I waited about to read it, and thought it good. So home, and the children tell me that the schools that they attend had their radios set to listen to the proceedings, and to the President, which I think is a good thing, in especial as most of the teachers, and most of the parents of the Weston and Fairfield children voted for Mr. Willkie, who, by the way, some of my anti-Roosevelt friends have washed their hands of because he talked yesterday to the President at the White House.

Thursday, January 23

To the train of a springlike morning, and to the office for a tiny time, and thence to the office of the National Labor Relations Board, and Mr. L. Gannett and I gave what amounted to a history of American journalism. So to a thronged party at N. Bel Geddes's, and met my wife there, *apud ceteros*, as the kids studying the accusative case have it. So had supper, and thence with my wife to see "Lady in the Dark," a mighty well-acted play, and the best ever I saw Miss Lawrence, albeit there were many places that I, and I alone, found tiresome. For some it reminded me of "Merrily We Roll," and I wondered whether "Dream Girl" might not have been a better title, much of the play being concerned with dreams and the psychoanalytic significance of same. So I down town and to bed, but did not fall asleep for a long time, either because of or in spite of reading Erle Gardner's "The Case of the Sulky Girl."

Thursday, January 30

Up with a bound, and to look at the thermometer, which was at zero, Fahrenheit, and I wondered whether Hitler would deem it an act of war if we ceased to use the name of that German physicist. So the house being warm, it was hard to believe it was a cold day, but it was, and in Bridgeport they do say it was the coldest since 1904, which I find it hard to credit. This day the President is 59 years of age, and there will be no difficulty ever remembering his age, he being but 25 days younger than H. Swope, who is, as F. Sullivan might say, an inveterate devotee of the sport of kings, and as I once called him in a spirit of fun, the king of sports.

Monday, February 3

All this day at work at some versification, and again discovered that it is the only work that is not irksome, and among other matters I thought of remaking an old verse of Gelett Burgess's:

> I'd rather be torrid than froze;
> I'd rather write poems than prose;
>   And as for th' afflatus,
>   Though skidding its status,
> I'll be awfully sad when it goes.

Read this day Miss Jan Struther's book of poems, and I fear that the popularity of them will be low, forasmuch as they all make sense, they rhyme, and they are short. For:

> Brevity and lucidity
>   Are what nobody buys;
> But have ponderous turgidity
>   And you will win the prize.

Lord! I vow some day to write a poem about the more ponderous the poem the heavier the dough.

Thursday, February 6

To the office before noon, and so home by daylight, what with the lengthening of the days. So in the evening I listened to the Town Meeting, and to show what a free country this is, Mr. George Sokolsky mentioned "putting the President in his place." Lord! if I had been there I should have told him that the people of the United States had put him in his place for the third time, and that his place is 1600 Pennsylvania Avenue, Washington, D. C.; and his place is also that of Commander-in-Chief of the Army and Navy. A lot of silly talk going about concerning the identification tags to be used by everybody in training, some saying that means that the boys are about to expire, although it means no more than that everybody who hath a policy of life insurance cannot possibly live another year.

Tuesday, February 11

By train to the city with R. Irvin, he in a merry mood, and tells me how his daughter Barbara went dancing in Newtown, and that midnight is deemed an early hour for the youth of that village. So read how the Mayor and Mr. Willkie testified this day before the Foreign Relations Committee, and the Mayor said of his appointment of Judge Herbert F. O'Brien that he had made some excellent appointments in his time, but that when he made a mistake it was a beaut, which observation I commend to the next compilers of any book of quotations. So home and tried to work out the formula for arithmetical progression, but albeit I remembered the formula, I had forgot how to work it. I know that the sum equals half the number, multiplied by the sum of the first and the last number in the series. But my boy, who still

is in Factoring, thinks that Progression is black art. So to
bed, with surds and indices dancing through my head, and
I wish that I had my old Hall and Knight's Algebra.

Thursday, February 13

I read this morning a good piece in the Saturday Review
of Literature called "Poetry and Poppycock," by Elizabeth
Jackson, clean as two hounds' teeth and three whistles,
about the phoniness of much poetry, especially modern
poetry, and of the silliness of the cryptic allusion. And it
occurred to me that a good name for all that stuff might be
Clutterature. Lord! what contempt some have for clarity
and lucidity, as though it were not harder to achieve than
obscurity. Home early, Tim having a fever, and I having
to read "Pecos Bill" to him till nine o'clock.

Sunday, February 23

Early up, and worked upon some verses, and then read
Jno. Kieran's "Nature Notes," and he makes the birds an
interesting subject, because he is interested in them. For
given the ability to write coherently, anybody who is
actually interested in a subject can communicate that
enthusiasm to his reader. So to the train to catch up Mr.
and Mrs. Sam'l Grafton, and so home to dinner, and found
Miss Dot Thompson there; and after dinner S. Chase come
in, and there was some good talk about the war, and, varied
as views were, there was agreement that the lend-lease bill
was right, and that, regardless of what Britain had been or
done in the past, she should now be helped to our capacity.
But I find that Mr. Grafton and Mr. Chase and Miss
Thompson, all writing down their convictions and opinions
on current matters, are great listeners, as opposed to those
who are so anxious to speak their views that they are merely

waiting for another view-expresser to stop. For this is truth eterne: Only the listeners learn.

Monday, March 3

Great talk in the city about Rob't Moses, who contendeth that museums are obsolescent, and that they should feel the breath of life along their keels, or words to that effect. All of which hath to do with his desire to move the site of the Aquarium from Battery Park to Bronx Park, which I am for, because I think that a man like Mr. Moses hath earned the right even to be mistaken; as I think Mayor LaGuardia and President Roosevelt also have earned that right. For no man who goes to bat, so to speak, many times a day, and always with the bright light of publicity upon him, and sometimes blinding him so that he drives off the road, now and then may make an error, and may even in his hurry mix his metaphors. Lord! I had liefer do a thousand things, and have nine hundred of them move toward the public good than do ten and have them emerge with a perfect score. To the city pretty late, and home again in my house before five in the evening, and watched the sunset skies for an hour, of great beauty, and I thought:

> When sun sets over Saugatuck,
> And Weston winds are o'er me
> So fond and fair, that otherwhere
> How can the world be stormy?

So in the evening wrote letters, and cast up some accounts, to find out how much I shall have to give to my country Friday week, and hoping that I may have enough to give, and whatever it is, this is the year that I shall begrudge it least.

Sunday, March 16

Up before eight o'clock of a sunny day, and read in the newspapers all the morning, save for some attempt to write

— 169 —

something, and after dinner I did go after it again, not without a little success. But there are two kinds of writer: one believes what he writes looks far better in print than when he thought of it, or even penned it; the other feels that his thoughts are excellent, but when printed they seem flat and obvious, in which latter class, Heaven help me, I am. This evening Anthony and I listened to Professor Rugg and to a man who objected to what he had written, though it seemed evident that the man had not read through a single book of Rugg's. I have read many of the Rugg books through, and far from seeing aught subversive in them, I deem them highly patriotick, and if any of my boys should turn out no good, it would be much more their parents' fault than that of any or every textbook they ever studied. And often the fault of a teacher, too, who may have an effect good or ill; for there is no subject that an interested teacher cannot make interesting, nor is there any subject that a bored or incompetent teacher cannot denature. Well I recall how absorbing Dr. Alderson made Mathematicks in all its branches; and how dull Prof. Earl Wilbur Dow made History. So crooned myself to sleep, longing for spring, and decided to write a poem, so up in the middle of the night, and wrote a note The Weston winter lasts until the dogwood blooms on Greenfield Hill, and hoped that I would not mislay the note before late in April.

Wednesday, April 2

Up betimes and to the office, and read that the German and Italian Governments, albeit it is about time to call it the German Government, protested the seizure of the Italian and German ships in our ports, the seizure being not only legal, but so necessary that I think it should have been accomplished at least a month ago. But I think the legality is what Hitler does not like, forasmuch as if we lied and cheated, he would probably send us a note saying, "That's more like it." So met my wife on the train, and drove her home, and after having seen the play last night, I was gladder than usual to see the children. So to bed, reading in "In This Our Life" until midnight, amazed for the tenth time at the unfailing vigor, wit, and compassion of Ellen Glasgow.

Wednesday, April 9

Up early of a pretty morning, and to the village to do some chores, and read some pieces about the school books written by Dr. Harold Rugg, some of it so intolerant as to make me doubt that those who prated the most about liberty and democracy gave any thought to the meaning of the words. And I know that many of those who talk about those books know nothing but what they have read in excerpts, and I would put Dr. Rugg's veneration for the country far ahead of that of his detractors. And I was minded of the days when an editor I worked for was violently opposed to the performance of "Mrs. Warren's Profession," and somebody asked him whether he had seen it, or read it, and he said that he didn't have to see it, or read it, that he was opposed to any such matters. So in the evening to see the pupils of the Unquowa School play "A Midsummer Night's Dream," a few of the players speaking clearly, but most so untrippingly on the tongue I had as lief the town-crier spoke the lines. Such as saying "Peermus" instead of "Pyramus." So home, and Tim having heard Shakespeare for the first time, said "I willeth helpeth you to putteth the car in the garageth."

Saturday, April 19

Up by times, and with F. Wierk and two of my boys riding through the country on a fine warm day, and fetched up at Washington, in Connecticut, and had a talk with

Mr. T. Van Dyke, who seemed to me to be a man of unostentatious erudition, and so stopped there for an hour, and so on, and had a mighty poor luncheon by the roadside. So on to Massachusetts, to Old Deerfield, and saw the school there, and a mighty fine place, too, and thence to Amherst, and had dinner, and thence to a cinema theatre, and saw "The Sea Wolf," a good thing too, I thought, and so all to an inn for the night.

Sunday, April 20

Up pretty early, and so found D. Morton the teacher and poet, and good at both, I will be bound. And he had us to breakfast, and so out in the pretty country again, very warm, and to Watertown, and saw the Taft School there, which seemed far finer physically than things were in my day at Ann Arbor, when my total weekly expenses were $5.50, including three meals a day at Mrs. Norton's on Ann Street, and two of them not bad, neither. Yet I am not one to say that what was good enough for me is good enough for my sons, because even the Remsen's Chemistry I used is obsolete, and how many elements have been discovered since I studied it I do not know, save that I never have heard of most of them. So on to Wallingford, and walked about, and found Arthur Otis, Hurlbutt '40, and talked to Mr. Geo. St. John a bit, and so drove home, and got there before eight o'clock, and went pretty early to bed, and finished reading "Flotsam," which shows how far-reaching the Gestapo is, and the trouble that utterly innocent persons are in who seek to cross any European border.

Thursday, April 24

A little cooler this morning, but I wore no surtout, lest I be tempted to go to the baseball game, and I knew that it would be too cold, so I worked the whole day, and with some zest, too, and on the way home I wrote some rhymes on the train, and vowed to do such things more frequently, for it is the only place where no telephone communicates with my cell, nor is there any passenger who asks for help with his algebra or his Latin. Home before seven, and so to supper, of a lamb stew, which I was holpen thrice to, and thenafter, behind a locked door, did an hour's work, albeit Tim knocked, and said, "This is important," so I opened the door, and he tells me that the Yanks are leading the league tonight. Yet I could not but think this is the only nation in which even a child considers that important.

Sunday, June 8

Early up, and drove my boys to Darien, and there met B. Karloff, and his wife and Mrs. Colston, a Baltimore lady that tells me that she knoweth Hugh Young, my old Neufchâteau buddy, who drove us to Forest Hills, and there saw F. Perry trounce J. D. Budge, and then two of us who were true to each other as the stars above did Mr. Karloff and Mr. D. Taylor wrong but albeit all of us were playing on turf for the first time, we were doing it to help Britain. So met Karl Behr, and we recalled the day he beat Maurie McLaughlin at Seabright, and how sad I was that such a thing could be.

Tuesday, June 10

All day at work, and mighty perturbed over the sinking of the American flagship, Robin Moor, by the Nazis, and what is to come of it I do not know, but I doubt that it will mean war for us; which reminds me of the wager that I made last January with an officer of the Navy that we should not have declared war before July 1. So home by an early train, and so took three children to hear their brother Tim make a graduation address of gratitude to his teachers and to the parents, and spoke with so much feeling that a child of about three years of age was moved to audible tears, which caused my boy to forget a sentence. So drove home, and he noted that he had forgot his diploma, so drove him back to get it, and so to bed before eleven.

Monday, June 23

Up, and find that most of those I saw and spoke to considered the Russian invasion by Germany a good thing, temporarily at least, for the United States and Great Britain in that it would give them a little breathing space to get more implements of war ready. The Soviet's Foreign Commissar Molotoff has predicted that the Nazis will be crushed by his Red Army, but it is hard to know what to believe, or what is said honestly or merely for advertising purposes.

* * *

PHILOSOPHY I

The principles of Horatio Alger, Jr.,
Are likely to roon yer.

The morals of G. A. Henty
Are spurious but plenty.

The author of "Elsie Dinsmore,"
Martha Finley, made my sins more.

To horse I've always done my duty
Ever since I read "Black Beauty."

Alcoholic love left me flat,
Notwithstanding "The Rubiayat."

I lived according to Karl Marx,
And wearied of sleeping in the parks.

I was a sucker for Schopenhauer,
And boy! did I find existence sour!

Coúe's tenet I found I curse;
Day by day I got worse and worse.

I studied those books with a mind so free
That now I haven't any sort of philosophy.

* * *

*(The next series of paragraphs appeared in The Conning
Tower 1938–1939)*

We have no quarrel with the "Advertising Makes Work"
slogan that the sloganeers have created. But work makes
advertising, too. Some of the blame for advertising's slump
is placed on labor, Roosevelt, the Republican Party, the
radio, and what not. How about overadvertising? How about
trying to sell people what they don't want if they had the
money, which they haven't got because they bought what
they didn't want?

* * *

When Dr. Ruth Andrus suggested to the N. E. A. that
there was a need for friendly teachers, that many teachers
didn't like children, she was, it seems to us, naïve. Any
teacher that, after a few years of association with children,
can continue to like them, deserves beatification. For there
is no gratitude in children, or in their parents. Usually when
a child fails to "do well" in school, the child and the parents
blame the teacher; if the child does well, it is the child's
fault. Except in rare instances, the teacher can't win.

* * *

Or a teacher likes children; and likes teaching. What goes
through her mind year after year on the last day of school?

She has become attached to her pupils and interested in their development. With a hoot and a yell, they burst from the cell, or schoolroom; next year they go to the next teacher, or into the so-called world. And the chances are that she doesn't know what becomes of them; next year's crop occupies her attention; and so on.

* * *

The big campaigns are in the future, so candidates are not making that phony appeal to Every Thinking Man. If voting were thus restricted, the vote would be infinitesimal.

But the treasured Times makes an even narrower appeal. "In these circumstances," it says, "every far-sighted citizen will accept the challenge offered and do his best to defeat the new Constitution as a whole." It seems to us that the taking of the next census would be simplified if a census were to be taken of only All Thinking Men and All Far-Sighted Citizens. . . . Of course, the candidate means that he is a Thinking Man, just as the editorial writer means that he is a Far-Sighted Citizen.

Our hope is that every unthinking man and every near-sighted citizen will agree with the Thought and Far-Sighted-ness expressed in the preceding paragraph.

Our guess is that a newspaper whose readers would include all the unthinking and near-sighted in town would have to install a lot of new presses.

* * *

It always interests us when we read that somebody has gone abroad to study conditions, traffic, labor, or what not. Mr. Frank Gannett, for example, who addressed the Young Republican State leaders at Saratoga Springs, was described as "recently returned from a study of labor conditions in England." How does a publisher of newspapers, Republican or Democrat, study English labor conditions? Whom does he see? Whom does he ask? Does he ask a few employers how things are? Does he mingle, on a fraternal basis, with laborers? Will laborers talk frankly to an Employer, theirs or somebody else's? We don't know; but our experience is that few employers come clean to the help, and few employees come clean to the boss. Of course, we haven't "studied" the question; we'd like to study labor, or bicycle-riding, in Bermuda. . . . We don't know Mr. Gannett's age, but it is probably more than thirty. In the days when we studied—we quit forever at the age of eighteen—study meant 8 A. M. to 10 P. M., and even then coming to some classes Unprepared.

* * *

Sweet are the uses of advertisement—sweet, and often inscrutable. On the local hoardings is depicted a young woman with a tennis racket, obviously playing. "It's fun," the legend says, "to be saving." The advertiser is the East River Savings Bank. What is the young woman saving? Her strength? Her beauty? Has her bank deposit enabled her to purchase a tennis racket, and a costume? The whole thing beats us, 6—o.

Besides, we deny that it is fun to be saving. It is fun to be prodigal. Go to the butterfly, thou parsimonious sluggard; consider her ways and get wise.

* * *

Thomas Wolfe's death leaves a wide gap in American letters. Since his "Look Homeward, Angel" we have not had the patience to read him; we couldn't get through "Of Time and the River." But his ambitions were as colossal as he was physically. It seemed to us that his lack of humor was also immense; that lack that so often goes with genius. For frequently the possession of humor keeps a novelist from reaching the stars; he has so strong a sense of the ridiculous that he fears to soar, lest somebody might shout "Hey, what are you doing way up there?"

* * *

"I never developed great excitement over Czecho-slovakia's fate," wrote George Sokolsky in yesterday's Herald Tribune. "Somehow, small nations seem to me a fearful economic waste." They are something like poor people, an economic waste in that they are a charge on the state. The thing to do, anybody can see, is for small nations to cease being an economic waste; let them become large nations, just as poor people can obviate their poverty by becoming rich.

* * *

"No meat for me," said the older boy. "I'm a vegetarian." "Give me some," said the younger boy, "and some more spinach and prunes. I eat everything. I'm a totalitarian."

* * *

President Kamal Ataturk, the papers said yesterday, is a poker player. We have often wondered how it would be to play poker with a dictator. Probably if he doesn't like his hand he calls it a misdeal; and maybe you pay when you lose, and when he loses he doesn't have to settle.

One can imagine playing with Hitler. You have four nines. You bet, and he calls, showing a pair of deuces. You throw your cards away, saying, "That's good, Fuehrer."

* * *

"I'll bet anybody even money," said Mr. Henry Ford, "that there'll never be another war." Mr. Ford could have got odds, but if he wants even money he's on. We'll bet him one 1940 Lincoln. Mr. Ford may be one of those reckless gamblers; maybe he'd like to bet that he, and the other passengers on the Oscar II, got the Boys Out of the Trenches by Christmas, 1915.

* * *

So this politician, at the end of a campaign, couldn't sleep, so he began on the sheep enumeration business. But when he reached 602 he couldn't remember whether it was 602 or 702, but fell asleep. And he had a dream. And the papers had eight-column streamers, "Sheep Demand Recount."

* * *

SPRING: EASTERN WAR TIME

From Stonington to Stamford,
     From Colchester to Kent,
Magnolia and forsythia
     Tell that the winter's spent.

And early sings the phoebe,
     And later sets the sun,
And green on elm and maple
     Says that the winter's done.

And many a broken window
     In hovel and in hall
Tells that, till falls the darkness,
     The boys are playing ball.

* * *

BALLADE OF COMPARATIVE JOY

Fashioning verses is far from fun;
Even duller is penning prose.
Sorry his lot who sees the sun
Rise and set on a world of woes.
Powerless he to ease the throes

Of millions yearning for work and bread,
Still, though life is no thornless rose,
I'm happier than in a hospital bed.

Oftentimes my ideas are none;
Black are the days as a flock of crows,
And the heart within me weighs a ton;
The nights I wake, and the days I doze.
Yet, after all it's the life I chose,
And, though it keeps me barely fed,
And I'm worried about next winter's snows,
I'm happier than in a hospital bed.

I've kicked and screamed at the web I've spun—
A job with a start and never a close;
For a columnist's work is never done,
And the longer he's at it, the tougher it grows.
Toss a ton of salt on my "Ahs" and "Ohs";
I lie when I say that my life is lead.
Hating the job is the workman's pose;
I'm happier than in a hospital bed.

L'ENVO I

Nurses and doctors and all of those,
Gramercy, folks, that I am not dead.
Yet I shall yell, when Gabriel blows,
"I'm happier than in a hospital bed."

* * *

THE REAL NEW YORKER

Oh, I am the hero of this ditty;
A resident I of New York City.
I think that the rest of the world's a pest,

And I think that Cleveland is way out west.
At knowing the hot spots I'm adrert
And I once knew a fellow from Detrert.
Where every night club is I know
Although it is true that I never go.
I live in a one-room flat that's swell,
Ten feet from the Seckind Avnoo L.
I spent two weeks up at Kezar Lake,
But the country quiet kept me awake.
I don't often go to see a show,
But I've got an elegant radio.
No symphony concerts and all such things—
Give me a band that knows the swings.
And say, the trouble with this here nation
Is people don't care about education.
A college man? Nay, nay, old socks,
I'm a grad of the College of Good Hard Knocks.
And I'll tell you this, beyond any doubt,
When you leave New York you're campin' out.
I don't read books any more, but, say,
I read the gossipers every day.
Yop, hero I of this little rhyme,
A dweller in New York City I'm.

* * *

"THE LORE SHE BROUGHT ME,"

*Or: A Few Things That I Have Learned In 25 Years of
New York Newspaper Work*

1. That the newspaper business is not so cruel as other businesses are said to be, or as it is supposed to be. Editors and publishers are more sentimental, and more tolerant toward incompetence, than employers in any other business or profession.

2. That many newspaper men ought not to be in the business, and that few non-newspaper men ought to be in it.

3. That the best and the best-paid reporters don't get paid half of what I think they deserve.

4. That young men who take up Journalism in order to get into close touch with life don't get into close touch with life, because they look upon life—and Journalism—as slumming.

5. That the ratio of crooked publishers and owners to crooked reporters is fifty to one. For crooked read corruptible, and make it one hundred to one.

6. That the business office and the editorial office hate each other. The business office's hate is founded on contempt, and the editorial office's on fear.

7. That most newspaper men care more about pleasing an editor or a publisher than about serving the reading public. This is usually waste effort, as the person to be pleased or flattered usually is too stupid or too indifferent— and sometimes too honest and intelligent—to be affected.

8. That copy readers—headline-writers, that is—have more influence on contemporaneous opinion than editorial writers have.

9. That it is easier to get a hundred dollars a week extra when you are signing on for a new job than to get a five-dollar-a-week raise when the job is a year or more old.

10. That the copy reader, joked about for his short-word clichés—Grills, Flays, Foe, Urges, Aids, Grid Tilt, etc.—has exerted a tremendous effect, mostly good, on the language.

11. That, in spite of the fact that editors tell reporters to write concisely, most stories are overwritten. Almost every important story is told at least twice.

12. That newspaper inaccuracy seldom is justly attributable to haste; oftener it is the fault of sloppy-mindedness,

a common trait in all businesses. But reporters—and newspapers—are incredibly more accurate than the persons who tell them stories full of alleged facts.

13. That—and I think the late Bert Leston Taylor told me this when I told him that I was doing some reporting for the New York Sun and that I found every assignment fascinating—there are no dull stories; there are only bored reporters. And that a reporter's life-preserver is his curiosity. Let him lose that and he might as well go into the press-agent business; or, if he prefers, the profession of Public Relations Counselor.

14. That there are five times as many well-written stories in the New York newspapers of today as there were in the Good Old Days of 1885–1900.

15. That a newspaper man must be willing to sacrifice his friends; that a newspaper man of twenty-five years' active work in the editorial room counts any friends at all as so much velvet.

16. That most newspaper reference libraries are disgracefully inadequate.

17. That the only newspaper editor whose praise or censure I ever believed with one-hundred-per-cent faith was Mr. Selah M. Clarke, in happier days managing editor of the still happier Sun.

18. That "blamed it on" is wrong.

19. That plurality is the lead of a candidate over one other; majority, over all others.

20. That anthracite is a noun, and only a noun.

21. That it's the Pennsylvania Station, but Grand Central Terminal.

22. That it is wrong to say "on either side of the street" when you mean on each side.

23. That eastern telegraph editors think that a telegram from Ann Arbor, Michigan, is a mistake of the telegrapher's,

so they change it to Ann Harbor. Frequently it is allowed to stand that way.

24. That "hectic," "transpire,"and "meticulous" don't mean what reporters think they do.

25. That it is Pittsburgh, Wilkes-Barre, and world series.

26. That it took me years to get a composing-room to let the serial comma stand in my stuff: Paints, oils, and varnishes instead of Paints, oils and varnishes.

27. That business men always ask newspaper men whether that is *all* that they do, no matter what it is.

28. That nothing makes me so angry as to hear somebody say, "That is too good for a newspaper; it is good enough for a magazine." I never have seen anything too good to appear in a newspaper.

29. That not one editorial writer in five feels passionately about the subjects editorial writers, in type, profess to have violent convictions about.

30. That most editors, publishers, and reporters know almost nothing about typography.

31. That most editors, especially outside of New York, have a contempt for amateur sports—golf, lawn tennis, polo—with the result that sport pages are topheavy with boxing, racing, and baseball news. The golf and tennis budget is disgracefully small.

32. That newspapers devote too much space to politics.

33. That there are three ways, disproportionately to the small expense, in which a newspaper can increase its revenue and good-will:

a. By employing efficient, courteous, and well-spoken telephone operators.

b. By having courteous and intelligent—therefore well-paid—persons in the reception-room, so that visitors to the staff will not be made to feel like intruders.

c. By paying non-staff contributors upon acceptance instead of upon publication, and by replying to every letter on the day of its receipt.

34. That the weather forecasts are printed as furnished by the Weather Bureau of the United States Department of Agriculture, and are not made up or guessed at by the newspaper, although most readers continue to say, "The paper says Rain," and—when it doesn't rain—"The paper is always wrong."

35. That criticism, literary and dramatic, is honest and, considering the physical difficulties under which it is written, exceptionally competent. According to a critic's length of service, it first infuriates, then amuses, and finally bores him when somebody asks him what he *really* thought of the play or the book.

36. That advertising exerts a good and a bad influence on American journalism. I think the influence more bad than good. But the fear of the loss of advertising is exaggerated. I still believe that an intelligently fearless newspaper would be a community's greatest benefit. It would also make its owner wealthy, if he could afford to risk a few million dollars for five years.

37. That information is the greatest thing that a newspaper has to sell. Opinion and entertainment are incidental and secondary.

38. That, except on pay-days, I always have considered myself shamefully underpaid. I have felt that there wasn't money enough to pay for that skillful, difficult, and important work. And on pay-days, regardless of what my salary has been, I always have felt that no human being could do work that was worth so princely a wage.

39. That the fact that morning papers are now purchasable before midnight—sometimes at eight o'clock—and

evening papers are on the street as early as 8 A. M.—is a bad thing for journalism. It makes for canned and syndicate stuff, and makes reporters hurried and careless.

40. That the use of "early today" or "late last night" is an intent, sometimes unconscious, to deceive the reader into thinking that the event occurred about ten seconds before the instant of publication. Sometimes it is difficult to be accurate as to the time of an accident, but I know that readers want to know exactly how "early this morning" eleven persons were injured in the subway, or on an "L" train. Thousands of persons want to know whether their husbands or wives or sons or daughters could possibly have been on that train. Early today means 12:01 A. M. to some; it means 11.30 A. M. to others. Thousands of readers will believe that they just avoided taking that train. My first big newspaper experience was the Iroquois Theatre fire; I learned then that at least one hundred thousand Chicagoans said that they had tried to get tickets for that fatal matinée performance, or were on their way to the theatre, or refused invitations to see the show that afternoon. I think that newspapers ought to identify railroad trains, in accident stories, and identify them in the first paragraph—what time the train left where, and when it was due where. I think that when possible the makes of motor cars involved in accidents should be printed. If a man possibly drunk says that the brakes were faulty, or that the steering gear wouldn't work, I wouldn't print the name of the car, however.

41. That the reporter's opinion in a news story hurts it ten times to once that it helps it.

42. That nobody is so distrusted in a newspaper office as the comedian—the columnist, the comic-strip artist, or the satirical cartoonist.

43. That most editors are infantile about letters; a single letter praising or dispraising a story, a picture, or a feature

has more weight with the editor than his own conviction as to the excellence or demerit of the piece in question.

44. That a stodgy, prosy piece of verse will receive ten times as much praise from office mates, from the owner down, as a piece of first-rate light verse.

45. That newspaper work is no training, in itself, for good writing; it will not make a first-rate writer of a poor writer.

46. That newspaper work is no destroyer, in itself, of good writing; it will not make a second-rate writer of a first-rate writer.

47. That among the things I wouldn't do for any salary is to work for W. R. Hearst, although I never had a chance to find out whether I was honest on that point.

48. That if I had enough money to live on, and live well on, I'd quit the newspaper business tomorrow; that otherwise I would rather earn twenty-five thousand dollars a year in journalism than one hundred thousand dollars in anything else that I ever heard of.

* * *

A PSALM OF MODERN LIFE

[Versified calls to be up and doing are becoming shriller every day; no longer the sweet Longfellow cadence.—Ralph Thompson, in the Times, on books of verse by C. Day Lewis and Paul Engle.]

Tell me not in cadenced numbers
    Life is but a rosy dream,
For the bard is dead who slumbers,
    And things are just what they seem.

Life is false, and life is phony,
    And the grave is near at hand;
Rhyme and metre are baloney
    In a liberty-loving land.

No enjoyment—only sorrow
　Is the single theme for verse;
But to write that each tomorrow
　Finds us write a little worse.

Art is bunk, and Time's a shackle,
　And our hearts are soft and weak.
Work's a thing for slaves to tackle,
　Concentration's for the meek.

In the world's uneven battle,
　In the futile fight for life,
Be not anybody's chattel,
　Be a pauper in the strife.

Trust no persons, howe'er pleasant;
　Work is for the workingman;
Idle, idle for the present;
　Wait for Mr. Townsend's plan.

Lives of "great" men all remind us
　We can make our lives a flop,
And, departing, leave behind us
　Fingerprints for every cop.

Thumbprints that perhaps another
　Member of the snarling men,
Blaming no one but his mother,
　Seeing may lose heart again.

Let us then be down-and-outers,
　Knowing we can't fight our fate;
All defeatists and misdoubters,
　Learn to belabor and to hate.

* * *

Great enthusiasm is reported at the Dewey meetings, and great enthusiasm is reported at the Lehman meetings. In all newspapers the reporting is honest, though the headlines usually stress the publisher's political leanings. Our plan for cutting down audiences, and therefore campaign speeches with their verboseness, is this: Charge one dollar admission to mass meetings; the crowds would melt away, feeling that they could do a lot better with a dollar. But if the crowds at a dollar a head were sizable, there would be a lot of money for campaign expenses.

At Yonkers on Monday night, for example, the Governor, in the first minute, said, "When you strip this campaign down to bedrock there is just one issue: Do the people want to elect as chief executive of the State a prosecutor or do they want to elect a Governor? And then he went on for two columns. If he was stripping the campaign to bedrock— and whether that is a metaphor taken from the stripping or the mining industry we don't know—why didn't he sit down at once?

A good many of us would vote for a man who began, "Accustomed as I am to public speaking, I know the futility of it. Voters, I thank you."

* * *

When it was announced that Mrs. Pearl Buck had won the Nobel Prize for Literature, she was quoted as saying that, now that she had won all that money, she would be able "To devote myself to writing books I want to write. Fewer short stories will need to be written." This, it seems to us, is a nonsequitur. If she means that she has written short stories that she didn't want to write, we wonder what the possession of about $40,000 will do to keep her from writing them, what the necessity of writing short stories is or was, and whether she has written any books that she didn't want to write. We doubt the last.

If a writer suddenly got $40,000 and said that it would obviate the necessity of writing at all, we could believe him or her. There is something in the compulsion that drives a writer to putting words on paper, but that it is enjoyable is something that we don't believe. Financial independence is the goal of lots of writers, though the term is elastic; for one it may mean $1,500 a year; for another the acquisition of a million dollars or more. Any millionaire who dislikes our writing so much that he will give us one million dollars can have a contract that never again will we write a word for publication. . . . Do we hear half a million?

* * *

Sign of winter: Putting the tennis racket up in the unheated attic.

* * *

It was a great tribute that the West Chester, Pa., Daily Local News gave to Mark Sullivan. That was the paper that gave him his first job. But we submit that we are a more indispensable journalist than Mr. Sullivan. For the West Chester Daily Local News, despite his defection from its staff, still is in existence. When we leave a newspaper's staff, the sheet seldom survives the shock. Our first paper, the Chicago Journal, is out of existence. So is the New York Evening Mail. So, as such, is the New York Tribune. And where is The World?

* * *

What the world needs, according to Mr. Herbert Hoover, is new faith, new morality. Why not upsweep the old morality, and have the old faith lifted?

* * *

Years ago in The World we selected our all-American football team. We still think that it could beat any other team. With a change or so, it follows, all the colleges being authentic:

Hand of Providence
Attar of Rose
Destruction of Carthage
Cedars of Lebanon
Land of Goshen
Diet of Rice
Quality of Mercer
Shouts of Defiance
Grist of Mills
Sway of Queens
Dissolution of Union

Substitutes: Hard, Knox; Dead, Centre; Precious, Jewell.

And five or six contribs offered:

Crossing of Delaware
Lump of Lehigh
Hart of Maryland
Maid of Athens
Bells of St. Mary's
Hat of Stetson
Wealth of Ind.
Crow of Wooster
Sun of York
District of Columbia
Pillars of Temple

Substitutes: Christmas, Carroll; Musty, Yale; Gimme,
De Pauw.

* * *

Times have changed since the old keep-at-it days. Once we were taught that the longer you held a job, the more competent you became; that keeping at the job led to advancement. This is the Rolling Stone Age. Mr. Rexford Tugwell had a government job; he resigned and went into the

molasses business. How good a molasses man he was we
don't know, but now he is a member of the Mayor's Committee on Housing Legislation. Jimmy Roosevelt was in the
yeast business; he then went into insurance; he then became
his father's secretary; and now he is a motion picture executive. Sadly, this moss-covered stone concedes the rollers are
right.

* * *

A fanatic for truth in advertising, we demur at Macy's talk
about a $15.97 poker table. "Designed for eight players,"
it ends, "and riotous fun." As one who has set in many an
eight-handed game, we say that eight of them can't have
riotous fun; if seven have r. f., the eighth player must have
a terrible time. In the average eight-handed game, there are
seldom more than five who have riotous fun.

* * *

The debate on "Do We Have a Free Press?" between
Secretary Ickes and Mr. Frank E. Gannett, owner of the
Gannett chain of papers, was a true debate, it seemed to
us, and not one of those canned affairs. It seemed to us that
Mr. Ickes had all the better of it. He said, in effect, that the
press is not dictated to by any political power or party, it is
influenced, too much he believes, by financial affiliations
and the influence of advertisers. No doubt about it, in spite
of some courageous exceptions. Purity, as we understand it,
is unknown, for that would include not only the ability to
print the truth, but to know what the truth is.

The Secretary cited the fair-mindedness of the Chicago
Daily News, whose publisher, Frank Knox, though he ran
for Vice President on the Republican ticket, allowed "a
column to criticize the Republican campaign and he printed
it in his column when he said that he did not think that
Frank Knox himself would make a good President." Be

fair, Mr. Secretary. Why not say that the columnist was Howard Vincent O'Brien?

We never had a boss run for office, but we rush to say that we never had one that would have made a good President. We've had times when we thought that he didn't know much about publishing a newspaper. But we never had a boss who didn't let us say what we wanted to about the party or the candidate that the paper was politically hot for.

Newspapers are neither so black as painted by Secretary Ickes, nor as white as calcimined by Publisher Gannett. A newspaper is as black as it is printed, and that's about all. Of course, if you print a better newspaper than your neighbor, the town will beat a path to your door. For that reason, every publisher tries to print a better newspaper than his neighbor, who is his rival. One trouble is that publishers don't agree on standards of excellence . . . We wrote a piece once telling what we'd do if we owned a newspaper; but nobody said, "Here's ten million dollars; and when that's gone, you can have another ten." If we had ten million, we'd run a paper; if we had one million, we'd quit work and write letters to the editor, beginning "I disagree with your specious and verbose editorial."

* * *

Mr. Frank Gannett has denied Secretary Ickes's statement, which was: "Did you ever read in a newspaper a story about an elevator accident in a big department store that was written and displayed on the basis of its news value?" Mr. Gannett cites instances in Albany and Rochester. There are many such instances in New York papers, of elevator accidents in department stores, printed with details. Such an accident gets as much publicity, proportionally, as an accident on a non-advertising railroad or subway system. Competition, which means also that if you don't print it somebody else will, is a great ally of press freedom. Secretary

Ickes can cite a good many instances of venality and distortion of news; Mr. Gannett can cite even more instances of knighthood. The truth, as it seems to us, is that the press is free, but not free enough.

* * *

Six boys between the ages of nine and fifteen came to New York on Monday. They were chosen from among 25,000 contestants, in a contest sponsored by the Typical American Boy Association, and are alleged to be typical boys. Possibly the contest was open to all school children; but our guess is that it was wageable among only subscribers to the American Boy. We know at least six typical American boys. And our definition of a typical American boy is one who would so hate to be known as a typical American boy that he wouldn't even enter such a contest.

* * *

Yesterday was the anniversary of Shakespeare's birth. Connecticut observed it quietly at Windsor, Avon, and Stratford.

* * *

One way to coax the fans back to the ball parks would be to have the man running from third on his way to the plate, with "He's leaving third base . . . We now pause for station identifications."

* * *

It will be cold comfort to a fielder who makes a shoestring catch to know that though there are only 300 spectators at the ball park, millions are hearing the catch described. You can't touch your cap to your unseen public.

* * *

Congress can't impair the freedom of the press, but General Hugh Johnson said there was nothing in the Constitution to prohibit the President from attempting to intimidate the press. How can the President intimidate the press? Off-hand, we don't know anybody who intimidates the press but some of the publishers who talk largely about the freedom of the press. Some of them want to intimidate the President, if it comes to that; and some of them want to intimidate the President's opponents.

"There is," said General Johnson, "a constant stream of accusation flowing from this administration that the whole press is perverting the news, unfair in editorial comment, and that it fills its columns with outright inventions without regard for truth." There is no such constant stream of accusation. But we accuse the press of often playing up some news, and playing down other news. That editorial comment is unfair is often true; but editorial writers are human beings, and it would be unfair to the human race to accuse them of everlasting and daily fairness. Why, now and then even this Turret of Truth grows a little tired of being fair; sometimes we indulge in a very orgy of violent prejudice, to keep our battery of fairness from becoming overcharged.

The newspaper publishers in town are shouting the battle cry of the freedom of the press. Their theme song appears to be "Red Hot Administration, Don't You Try to Menace Me."

Our freedom never has been menaced by any administration or any publisher. Why, never a publisher we worked for who wouldn't let us do a whole wide column six days a week. They even furnish scissors and paste, and for the rare occasions when we feel like writing a few words of our own, a lovely typewriter.

* * *

You can't tell anything about the quality of a man's brain by his headgear. If you could, there would be only three varieties of brain: soft, hard, and none.

* * *

This department is proud of Mr. Paul Patterson, president of the Baltimore Sun, but in 1903 the best-dressed $35-a-week copyreader who got his suits at Jerrems's that ever worked on the Chicago Journal. Mr. Patterson, though his speech was submerged in the accounts, said what to our mind was the truest of the many words spoken at the A. N. P. A. convention. "I am not worried," he said, "about the freedom of the press—it will be free as long as our government exists." He added that the press and the radio had worked together, and that news broadcasts create more demands for newspapers by educating the public in international affairs. A newspaper that tries to fight radio is King Canute trying to silence the ether waves.

* * *

Our guess is that whatever happens Poland won't win. Poland reminds us of the fellow at the racetrack. "How did you do?" he was asked. "Broke even," he said, "and boy! did I need it!"

* * *

"What the world needs," said Mr. Herbert C. Hoover, "is a return to sanity." Well, a good many of us lost ours some time between 1928 and 1932, so if Mr. Hoover knows a good brokerage house, we'll buy a nickel's worth. But not on margin; we'll take our sanity outright, or not at all.

* * *

THE FREEDOM OF THE PRESS

James Carrington was a newspaperman. He began as a reporter on The Appeal. He was a good reporter from the start. The editor-publisher, long before the talk of NRA and minimum wage, paid him $18 a week. By the time—five years—he grew to be the paper's best all-round reporter he was getting $95. The $5 was a raise. He had been getting $90;

The Gazette offered him $110; and Mr. Harrison offered him an extra $5 if he'd stay, hinting that there were chances for advancement for staff men.

Carrington worked six years more as reporter, during which time his $95 took care of a wife, acquired after the $5 raise, and two children.

And just as he had forgotten, with a cynicism that journalism breeds, all about Harrison's hint as to advancement, Edgar Maxwell Abbott, the chief editorial writer, aged sixty-nine and with The Appeal for fifty-four years, boy and man, died. They turned rule on the editorial page for his obituary editorial, written by Benjamin Clybourne, his assistant. "For the first time in fifty-four years," it began, "The Appeal goes to press this morning without the assistance of Edgar Maxwell Abbott. This page knew his work for thirty-six years. Few readers of this newspaper, few readers of this page, knew even his name." And so on—though many a reader said that an editorial writer has to die to win even one day's fame.

So Benjamin Clybourne was promoted to be chief editorial writer and Mr. Harrison asked Reporter James Carrington how he'd like to do editorials. He snapped at it. "Of course," said Harrison, "it is better paid work than reporting, and we'll take care of you." And they did. His pay was raised to $120. That was in 1927. In 1930, when cuts were the fashion, except in the unionized composing room, Carrington's pay automatically went to $108. "We can't cut the compositor's," Blevitch, the business manager, said. "And we have to save somewhere, so we have to shave editorial expenses." And in 1932 there was another 10-percent cut, and Carrington got $97.20. And in 1936 Carrington, writing at least two, sometimes three editorials a day, and having charge of the page for Monday's paper, was still getting $97.20 every Friday.

One afternoon in November, 1936, Mr. Harrison came to Carrington's cubicle, a thing he rarely did. Every morning there was a short, perfunctory editorial conference; subjects were assigned, partly to avoid duplication, partly to give the political man his subject, the sprightly writer his, and so on. Harrison seldom attended these conferences, so Carrington felt a slight thrill of elation when Harrison entered.

"Jim," said Harrison, "I assume you read the papers."

"Certainly," said Carrington.

"Well, then you have noticed how employment is increasing. There's at least a column a day of items telling that this concern has employed 2,000 more men, and that one 3,000, and so on. And this firm has increased pay 15 percent, and that one 10. Read the financial page?"

"Yes, sir. I read the whole paper, and most of the others."

"Well, then. Look at increased dividends. Resumption of dividends, all that. Now, I want you to write the leader tomorrow. Return of prosperity. Make 1929 look like nothing. Prosperity. Not around the corner. Here. And it is here, Jim. Put stuff into it; sincere, simple stuff. See?"

"I see," said Carrington. "But, Mr. Harrison, I can't write a sincere editorial about Prosperity when I've had two cuts. I got $120 when I started; now I get $97.20. That doesn't look like prosperity to me. I know the paper is making lots of money."

Harrison looked at Carrington as though he doubted his ears.

"Are you telling me you refuse to write an editorial that is true, and in line with the paper's policy of prosperity? I had more faith in your loyalty, Jim."

"I can't furnish all the loyalty," said Carrington. "How about yours to me?"

"Jim," said the editor-publisher, "I'm sorry. You've been

here about eighteen years. One of the family. I'm sorry. Jim, you'd probably be happier somewhere else. I'll send an order for two weeks' pay. Goodbye. Don't hesitate to ask me if I can do anything personally."

"You can personally go to hell," said Carrington. He took his hat, and left Harrison sitting in his little room.

* * *

WINTER-SPORTS NOTE

When icicles hang by the wall,
And snow upon the tree,
I hear the mating call
Of the not impossible ski.

* * *

Senator Vandenberg said, "We are engaged in an amazing effort, deliberately and unconsciously, to stretch an annual national income of $60,000,000,000 into an annual national income of $80,000,000,000 by spending the difference!" Well, ask a family man who has an income of $60 a month how he stretches it into an income of $80 a month; or better, ask him how he keeps from doing it.

"We must," said the Gentleman from Michigan, "leave the road to ruin while there is yet time." Of course, you will find those who think that we are not on the road to ruin. A wayfarer would ask a Republican, "Which way to ruin?" and the answer would be "Keep right ahead." Mr. Vandenberg's answer would be "Don't go there; it's a dead end. Detour sharp right to Vandenberg Road, turn sharp right and you'll find Prosperity Boulevard."

* * *

But most of us, if asked which way to Ruin and which way to Prosperity would have to answer, "I don't know. I'm a stranger here myself."

* * *

The other day we spoke of the anonymity of editorial writers. The day of publication we met an editorial writer who shall be, by request, nameless. "You're wrong about editorial writers," he said. "They get plenty of honor. Why, when an editorial writer dies, the whole office chips in to pay funeral expenses."

* * *

"So far as I can recall," wrote George E. Sokolsky, in the N. Y. Herald Tribune, "The President once read a Christmas story or something out loud over the microphone by Heywood Broun, highbrow columnist of the C. I. O." Now the President did read a Christmas column written by Heywood Broun, daily columnist of the Scripps-Howard papers. Mr. Broun is president of the American Newspaper Guild, which is a C. I. O. organization. Many co-workers of Mr. Sokolsky's on the Herald Tribune, for which he writes a weekly column, are members of the C. I. O. But it would be just as fair—fairer—for Sok to refer to one of the reporters as "The reporter of the C. I. O." Although Mr. Broun's belt is enormous, there is plenty of room to hit above it.

* * *

When MacLeish's "Conquistador" was published in 1932—it got the 1933 Pulitzer Award—we said that we didn't like the idea of the versification until we got into the story, and then felt its great beauty as well as its prosodic skill. And our platform then, as now, was:

> I do not like verse new and strange
> Because I am too old to change,
> And I think it takes more skill and time
> To say poetic things in rhyme.
> Opinions are written by dubs like me,
> But only poets write poetry.

* * *

Perhaps we were wrong, after all. For years we have contended that Hitler was the most humorless man in the world. He has placed the blame for the war on Great Britain. All of which discourages us. We slave away, we whittle a pleasantry to achieve perfection, we stay awake nights trying to think of the perfect comicality. And here is Der Fuehrer, tossing off a honey, tossing it off blindfolded and with his hands tied behind his back.

* * *

Our wish that the war would end reminds us of the baseball reporter who covered 154 games every season. At the opening game the first ball was pitched. "Ball one," said the umpire. "Oh, dear," yawned the reporter, "I wish the season was over."

* * *

Among words that have become, in some subtle way, to mean what they don't mean is "doubtless." Especially in criticism. When a critic says "This is doubtless a good play," or "Doubtless this is a great book," he means that in his opinion it is a poor play or a mediocre book. Or that no matter what the general opinion may be, he has misgivings about the verdict. Doubtless we are wrong about this.

* * *

HEYWOOD BROUN

1888–1939

Heywood Broun's passing leaves the biggest hole in American journalism that anybody living knows, or is likely to know. The impression of his personality, in print and out of print, is stronger than that of any other newspaper writer or publisher. He will be a legend, and a quoted writer, when the Pulitzers, the Danas, and the Greeleys are only names.

So much for prophecy. The gap that he leaves among those who knew him long and intimately is a vacuum—

permanent and ineffable. I have known Heywood longer than most of his friends; more intimately over a longer stretch of time than any of his other associates. It was a great joy and satisfaction that he was on the paper with Kirby and me, for it was to revive the vigorously and pugnaciously merry and happy days on The World. And on The Tribune, where he covered baseball and later did a three-day-a-week book column.

It wasn't until he came to The World, in 1921—he preceded me by six months—that his stuff began to soar to the stars. I was struck from time to time by what I imagined was Broun's brotherhood to Abraham Lincoln. For both had great humor, charm, and a deep and sincere feeling for the underdog. And many who knew Lincoln said that he was unfathomable. Not mysteriously, but deeply. And even to those of us who knew Broun best, he had depths that we never plumbed.

There was a strong Puritanism in Broun. I remember well days on The World, days when I would send a contribution up to the composing room, and mark it merely for type. Not so Heywood. Often he would print a letter from somebody—a letter a whole wide column long. But he would not insert "says so-and-so," and send the letter along. He would write, " 'I am in disagreement with you,' writes Charles Wood,"—and then he would type the whole letter, verbatim. It made him feel, he used to say, that he was working.

Shortly after he left The World in 1930, he joined the then unhyphenated Telegram. "Broun," said Mr. Roy Howard, his new boss, "is no mere jokesmith or phrase-carpenter, but an artistic debunker of political and official flapdoodle." Mr. Howard might have added "and journalistic." It was Mr. Howard's notion that Heywood could be more effective in type than in talk, more constructive in a column than in Congress. I thought, and still think, that what Mr.

Howard meant was that Heywood should devote all his powers to the column that Mr. Howard was paying him for. He didn't know Heywood, or understand him. For it never was extra-curricular work or play that interfered with the excellence of his column. I have seen him at a party, I have seen him at a poker game, when he said, "Deal me out a few rounds. Got to write a column." And in a room full of chatter he would write, in thirty minutes, a column that was as likely to be one of his best—which is no faint praise— as one that he spent four hours in writing.

I objected at the time that Roy Howard called him "no mere jokesmith or phrase-carpenter." For he was a poor jokesmith and never much of phrase-carpenter. Even now, the phrase that lost him his World job—that was a good one, too—is unremembered. He called Harvard, at the time the Sacco-Vanzetti appeal was rejected, "Hangman's House."

Broun was a debunker of any kind of pretentiousness— political, official, or literary. He hated bunk so much that he dressed carelessly and sketchily, because a man may be a fop and a villain still; he was the sort of man who would wear three hats in an elevator because he knew that some men would consider their entire duty and responsibility to women discharged when they removed their hats.

He hated injustice and intolerance; seldom did he dislike those he considered unjust or intolerant. He was a lion in print, but a lamb in his personal relationships. Men whom he attacked in print would invite him to lunch; he'd go, and the victim of his wrath would fall to his charm.

Heywood, for twenty years or so, must have earned lots of money. He cared less for money than anybody I know; he was the most avaricious person I knew. If he won $100 in a poker game, he'd settle for $90 cash rather than wait until the next afternoon for a check. Yet he would say that he had to get home to Stamford at midnight, call a cab to drive him home, and keep the cab until 7 A. M., in the hope that by that time he would be even, or ahead. How many persons who had no claim on him were supported entirely, or in part, by him nobody ever will know. Certainly if he spent more than $100 on his apparel it was not evident. When he was earning at least $50,000 a year we used to say that he looked like the 1904 Puck pictures of a Socialist.

For years seven or eight of us played poker on Saturday nights; the gathering got its name from the club in "Main Street," and later was expanded to the Thanatopsis Literary and Inside Straight Club. Broun was the originator of the elaborate joke, which began on a rainy night in his dining room, when he took a drink of what he called "a certain inferior liquor," and said "Any Port in a storm." His most recent one—it took him twenty minutes to tell—involved an overgrown papoose, whom the chief expelled, saying "You big; quit us." "That," he would explain, "is the origin of 'ubiquitous.'"

In the old days on the Tribune and the World Broun and I would talk about our obituaries. How it would just be our luck that we'd die too late for the first edition of those papers.

At the end, he was an evening paper man.

Peace to his soul!

* * *

(*The next series of paragraphs appeared in The Conning Tower 1940–1941*)

The newly elected president of Ohio State University is Mr. Howard L. Bevis, once a Judge of the Ohio Supreme Court, and once Director of Finance for Ohio. Maybe a state university feels that it has to have a president who knows a lot about money, for the Regents have to be talked to, so that money may be raised by taxation for the university. This department is old-fashioned enough to believe in a university president who is so interested in education that he wouldn't recognize a dollar if he met one on the campus.

In the Herald Tribune's story about Judge Bevis's election appears a sentence that we offer to Old Sam Grafton as a theme for an essay on what's the matter with American politics. "For many years," the story runs, "he served as a ward executive in Democratic politics in Cincinnati, taking part in the practical work of organization politics as a diversion from his more serious work in the University of Cincinnati." Why is politics a diversion? Still, maybe that's the matter with so-called education.

* * *

The President said that there is a lot of fun in his job, provided a man doesn't worry too much. The interpreters who are interlinear experts tell us that this means that the President would like four more years of that fun; though it may mean that it was fun, but it won't be fun much longer. We are as adroit an interpreter as the next fellow, and we take it to mean that he has enjoyed his occupancy of the White House, partly in spite of, and partly on account of what went with it.

It seems to us that a President, or his reputation, is made by the times and the temper of the people more than the other way around. What Millard Fillmore would have done in Lincoln's place nobody can say, though it is almost a fact of history that the nation was lucky to have had Lincoln. It is conceivable that some unborn Sandburg may write, in 2015 or so, the Life and Times of F. D. Roosevelt, with history's verdict that the country didn't know its luck during his Presidency.

When we said that the Presidents between Lincoln and

Franklin Roosevelt were lacking in humor, we meant as Presidents. For it seems to us that President Taft, out of office, may have been full of humor. We don't mean the ability to see or tell a joke, for Theodore Roosevelt was quite a one for that. But nothing in the public or official documents of Johnson, Grant, Hayes, Garfield, Arthur, Cleveland, Harrison, or McKinley, or the diaries of J. Q. Adams and J. K. Polk shows any humor. It never appeared to us that President Wilson had any; he was too fond of quoting a single limerick as an example of it. As to Presidents Coolidge and Hoover, they tell tales how they were humorous when you got to know them. Shedding a bitter tear, we doubt it.

It seems to us that the District Attorney is naïve. "Elections," says Mr. Dewey, in an article in the Republican Speaker, "are won by men and women who are informed and who believe in their party, its philosophy and its candidates, and who can and will carry an intelligent message to the voters in their respective district." Tut! Elections are won by men and women chiefly because most people vote against somebody, rather than for somebody. Not one in a thousand voters can tell you what the philosophy of any party is. What a candidate's philosophy is is easier: Get elected, regardless.

* * *

When Mr. John L. Lewis said that Miss Frances Perkins was "woozy in the head" and that she "would make an excellent housekeeper," he alienated, our guess is, most of the women in the land. In the first place, woozy-headed women hate being called woozy-headed; in the second place, every housekeeper will resent the implication that excellent housekeeping isn't an art, a science, and a career. For we never knew a woman who wasn't a good housekeeper. We know one who is such a thrifty housekeeper that she never throws away a newspaper, on the theory that she never knows when she might want to know what the weather forecast was for August 12, 1934.

* * *

Last night we had a dream. The envelope containing our income tax check was returned, with the notation, "Not known here. Left no address."

* * *

His tour through the country, Tommy Dewey says, convinced him that the country is going Republican, and is rapidly moving toward sanity and the return of the Republican party. Now a candidate, it seems to us, who has Great Confidence in the Great American people, ought not to imply that the country ever has been anything but sane, nor that those who may happen to vote the Democratic or the Socialist ticket are insane.

* * *

We'd like a candidate to come home from a tour of the country, and publicly say that neither he nor his party has a chance. Mr. Willkie's candor—he said that he had no chance of nomination—has won him thousands of adherents, if not delegates.

* * *

"I am glad," said Mrs. George Martin Dewey, the District Attorney's mother, "that he did not stick to his music but entered politics. It is a much nicer career being a lawyer. I think he can do more good as a lawyer than as a musician." Well, it is true that a musician—that is, a man whose main professional job is music—has no chance of nomination for the Presidency of the United States. And most American mothers would rather have a President for a son than a musician. But when she refers to law as a "nicer career" than music, we object. For that is highly debatable; our objection, which we hope will be sustained, is to the dictum that music is nicer than law. Who ever referred to the law as the Heavenly Maid? Who ever said that the man who had no law in his soul is fit for treason, stratagems, and spoils? Not even Longfellow said "And the night shall be filled with litigation." On the other hand, Dickens never said "Music is a ass, a idiot." Now when Mrs. Dewey says that she thinks that he can do more good as a lawyer than as a musician, we defer to an opinion that we do not share. We have known lawyers that do good, and some that have done harm. Probably we know even more lawyers than we do musicians, but the musicians we know are more fun, even when they are not playing, than the lawyers. The lawyers we know have done more good to themselves, financially, than the musicians have. And, including concert tickets and musical instruction for not-too-gifted children, and pianos and clarinets and zithers and harmonicas, we have spent even more on attorney's fees than we have on music.

Of course, music and the law are not mutually exclusive. While it is true that of our personal attorneys Mr. Morris Ernst is the only one who cannot carry a tune even feet first, our Mr. Morris Cooper, Jr., is an accomplished pianist, our Mr. Charles Riegelman is a baritone and a pianist, our Mr. Lloyd Paul Stryker can sing—and has sung in public—most of the Sullivan scores, and our Mr. Thomas R. Robinson of New Haven can sing and play, not to add his running into New York from time to time to the opera and to concerts. Well, Mrs. Dewey, the prosecution rests, except for the observation that an afternoon of music is pleasanter and "nicer" to listen to than an afternoon of the cross-examination of witnesses.

* * *

It appears that Mrs. Wendell Willkie gave her husband for his birthday (Feb. 18) "Abraham Lincoln: the War Years." How a reader of those four volumes can want to be President is beyond us.

* * *

The New Yorker and the Life biographies of Tommy Dewey are our authority for the humorlessness of Mr. Thomas Edmund Dewey. His Birmingham speech does nothing to make the biographers gulp their words. His implication that the President is playing cheap politics with the defense program, and his assertion that the National Defense Commission would, in effect, act as messenger boys for New Deal politicians who insist on keeping politics in the defense job would come better from a public officer who wasn't touring the country in his own behalf, and a District Attorney who stuck close to his desk and never went to sea.

* * *

Dean Gildersleeve of Barnard College, quoting Mr. Walter Lippmann, advised the graduates to face the world with clear eyes and a stout heart. Easier said than done, we imagine many a graduate thinking to herself. It is difficult to have either clear eyes or a stout heart at any time; it is harder now. And to have both great gifts is vouchsafed to few. We fail to remember a single word that was said to us, or even by whom, one day in a long past June, but probably it was something to the same effect. We thought of nothing but when the diplomas would be handed out—in what attic reposes that diploma now?—and whether the speaker would finish in time for us to get to a graduation party. And even though we read Mr. Lippmann's advice in the Herald Tribune before Dean Gildersleeve quoted it, we thought that here was a piece written by a clear-eyed, stout-hearted writer. The best most of us ever do, dear graduates, is to study the clear of eye and the stout of heart. For most of you will take, as most of the rest of us take, your clearness of eye and your stoutness of heart vicariously. These cloudy-eyed words are assembled by one whose heart, at the moment, wouldn't pass an examination for a one-year endowment policy.

* * *

Perhaps the boiling point of most of us is low these days. We simmer at the Times editorial that speaks of Hitler as "a neurotic soldier and an incompetent painter." As any psychiatrist will tell you, for next to nothing, all of us are neurotic; gather, the poet should have said, neuroses while ye may. But suppose Hitler was an incompetent painter? The story of success, especially American success, is full of examples of incompetence in one field, because or in spite of which, the failure went on to achieve conspicuous success in another. Theodore Dreiser was an incompetent reporter, and don't let him tell you different; Booth Tarkington's ability as an illustrator was less than brilliant; even Tommy Dewey's fame is not based upon his rendition of operatic arias. . . . Not that we don't wish that nothing could have swerved Hitler from his desire to be a painter, with maybe a little calsomining and paperhanging on the side.

* * *

There is one tradition that ought to be punctured beyond repair, although now there is no evidence of even a slow leak. That tradition is the method of election by the Electoral College. We'll believe in democracy when Presidents are elected by popular vote.

* * *

Writers should be frightened of the excess profits tax, if it ever is applied to individuals. For he cannot deduct for wear and tear on what Mr. Wodehouse's gentlemen call the

Old Bean, nor for keeping the Human Machine in the Pink, such as payments to doctors, dentists, and barbers. A writer's physical investment usually is one typewriter ribbon; or if he is a die-hard, enough ink to fill a year's supply of the fountain pen.

* * *

Constructive criticism, that good old cliché, is what Mr. Willkie wants to give the administration. It brings to mind something that Bert Leston Taylor said about T. R., and the constructive criticism of the Wilson administration. "After he has finished a bit of construction," he said, "it takes an hour for the dust to settle."

* * *

It seems to us that much of the talk we hear about American "softness" is bunk. If by that is meant that we are growing soft by not having to get up at 4 a. m. of a cold morning to milk the cows, we are soft. If we have heat at will by turning something on a thermostat instead of spending a lot of time with an old-style furnace, if we have hot water when we want it, if we ride in the subway for a mile or two instead of walking, we are soft. We are counseled by the advertiser to become soft by using an electric razor instead of the old-fashioned straight-edge razor. Does that make for softness? The 1941 automobiles may be driven, shift and all, with one finger; were we less soft when cars had to be cranked? Softness is a habit of mind and soul; and hardness, or courage, is the self discipline that if necessary would let all these comforts, which in the cosmic scheme are unimportant, go. But there is a difference between hardness and masochism; the mere wearing of hair shirts is no help to a nation. . . . As to what many persons would at first consider deprivations, you never know, to paraphrase it, what you can do without until you try.

* * *

REVISED

Tell me now in mournful numbers
Life no longer is a dream,
For the nation's dead that slumbers,
And things are worse than they seem.

* * *

There is much that we don't know about the problems of youth. But our guess is that dull and arbitrary teachers and dull and arbitrary parents have far more to do with causing youth to be rebellious, if not anti-social, than the so-called overliberal teachers. Youth, unless it has changed since last night, is harder to influence than many educational "experts" think. Kids nowadays think for themselves more than their parents do for themselves. Mighty few of us over forty, whatever Dr. Walter Pitkin thinks about it, are capable of independent thought or opinion.

* * *

Perhaps "love" is the word that, more than any other, means one thing to one person and another thing to another person. Even when one person says "I love you" the lovee has not the same notion of the word that is in the speaker's mind, and, possibly, heart. But there is considerable difference of meaning in the words "democracy" and "freedom." Those words are increasingly used by speakers and writers everywhere. And you have to know a lot about the users of these words, in order to arrive at their interpretation of them, and even then you are likely to use your own translation, which may be correct, or may be parasangs from what the writer or speaker means.

* * *

Of course, there are many who say that a daily columnist, which means a person who has six or seven full columns a week in a paper, doesn't really work, but that he would like other laborers to work six days a week for the period of the so-called—properly so-called—emergency. We know not what course others may take, but we never have been able to do it under a seven-day week, and some nights. Often we dream of Jeanie with the unfilled column. We dream that we have three minutes in which to write a column, have it set, read proof, and make it up. It would be pleasant to work five 8-hour days a week. To quit, in the middle of a syllable, if need be, when the whistle blew! And then some days, as if mere writing weren't enough trouble, there is a lot of clipping and pasting to do. It sounds easy, but it takes longer to find the shears and the paste for first-class stuff than it does to write third—all right, we won't argue—fourth-class stuff.

* * *

We were trying to help a boy who was doing some Home Work during the holidays; one of the questions was concerned with the difference between "legible" and "readable." It was easy. Example: "The Sun, with its new type face, is more legible, but no more readable."

* * *

Again to summarize the President's speech about national security, it seems that this still is Columbia, happy land where our fathers died, land of the pilgrims' pride, and that it will take an enormous lot of concentrated, unified work to let freedom continue to ring from every American mountainside.

For in the totalitarian and slave countries, they let freedom ring, too. But they don't answer the bell.

* * *

February 2 is only four weeks away, and it is pleasant to live in a country where the ground hog isn't afraid of his shadow.

* * *

Ambassador Phillips, it was reported, has brought to Italy a special personal message to King Victor Emmanuel. One pictures Mr. Phillips in Rome asking to be driven to King Victor Emmanuel's. "I'm afraid," the taxidriver might say, "you got to tell me where he lives, buddy. I don't know everybody in town."

* * *

AVE ATQUE VALE!

The Gazette, after fifty-two years of independent, crusading journalism, sold out. You might say, with justice, that it paid a terrific price for sentimentality. It was a Gazette tradition that nobody, in the editorial or business department, ever had been fired. It was the only paper in town that guaranteed the jobs of men who left the paper to enter the war—the Spanish-American War, and the World War. It did more than that. It paid the difference between the soldier's pay and the staff-man's salary. Prosperity was the Gazette's for fifty years; it was sincerely independent, and advertisers needed it even more than the Gazette needed them. It weathered the depression of 1929; and no cuts came, and nobody was fired.

Now, it so happened that the business office was peopled with dozens of old gentlemen; men who had been hired by Benjamin Wetherell himself, who had made the Gazette soar from the puny thing it was when he bought it in 1882 to the glorious heritage it was at his death in 1920.

The momentum of success or failure in a newspaper is a terrific force. A paper deservedly popular and successful may suddenly become unworthy of popularity and success; it takes years before the public, habituated to a paper it likes, becomes conscious that the clay of its idol's feet has permeated the whole body; just as, when a paper, long unpopular and unsuccessful, takes a sudden turn toward high standards of independent excellence, it takes years for the public to take it to its purchasing bosom.

The Gazette, then, developed business-office paralysis first; long accustomed to advertisers who begged for space, it was hard—it was impossible—for the relics of the easy prosperity of a dozen and more years ago to go after business. If it didn't surge in, something was the matter with business and business men. And it surged out, in droves. And the business office grew trembly when, for the first time, the expense exceeded the income. So—it couldn't do anything to the unionized composing room—editors and reporters, especially if hired since the Old Man's death, took salary slashes or got fired. The standards of the paper drooped; the advertising fell to a pitiful shadow. And then an enterprising young publisher offered to buy the name and the good-will— for three years after its toboggan the reading public, unaware or incredulous or hopeful, continued; circulation was almost normal, even at the end. The night the Gazette died was unforgettable; weeping there was, not only among the staff but all over town, for the paper had the admiration and affection of the whole nation.

Suddenly hundreds of men were out of work—reporters, editors, advertising solicitors, printers. Among those suddenly unemployed was Robert Bannerman, as uncompromising a critic of the stage as he was the ablest, soundest, and most entertaining writer among the critics. Yet, because of or in spite of this excellence, none was so poor to do him the reverence of offering him a job. All the papers had their critics; and monstrously unfair as newspapers often are, they seldom fire a competent department man in order to hire a conspicuously abler man. But when all looked darkest for Bannerman, James Spencer, the Courier's critic, youngest of the aisle-seaters, was killed by a taxi as he was hurrying from the theater to the Courier office. It so happened that before Bannerman joined the Gazette staff he had been successively reporter, editorial writer, and dramatic critic for the Courier. Fourteen years he had worked for the Courier when he left it, eighteen years before, for the larger wage the Gazette offered. When the Gazette folded, he went to see his first boss, the Courier's editor. Nothing in his line. Copy desk? Reporting? No, the staff was full up, but if anything turned up, etc. Bannerman, for thirty-two years, had heard editors tell aspirants that, and he couldn't remember that anybody ever had been let know.

And yet, in less than a week, here was Bannerman being let know. Let know by telephone. Spencer had stepped in front of a cab, rushing to the office from the theater, dashing out as the curtain was about to fall.

So Bannerman got the job, his old job. Elated at re-employment after his first panicky week of fear, he said nothing about salary. In fact, he arrived at the office at eight o'clock in the evening, saw the managing editor, who said, "Welcome home, Bob. Go over and cover the 'Why Not?' opening. We have a new deadline: 11:50 for the second edition." So Bannerman slipped into the well-known groove; he wrote his review, an excellent one, and at a little after midnight, after greeting some of his old friends on the city staff, went home, happy.

Next morning he went to the Courier office at ten. He went to see the editor-in-chief, Edgar Allen, an old friend. "Welcome home, Bob," he said. "Your stuff is better than ever." "Thanks, Ed. It's wonderful to be back again." "Now about salary," began Allen, "of course, you know the depression hit us pretty hard." "I know it must have," said Bannerman, "it put the Gazette out of business, and lots of good men out of jobs." "So," said Allen, "naturally, you've been in the game long enough to know that, we can't pay what you're used to. We'll pay you what you were getting when you left." "But, Ed," said Bannerman, "Spencer got three times that, I know." "He was with us eighteen years," said Allen, "and he would have had to take a big cut at the expiration of his contract. We aren't making any more contracts right now," he added quickly. "Who knows what's going to happen in Washington? So go on and get out a Sunday piece. Might stick in something about how much Spencer'll be missed in the theater, and so on. O. K.? Of course, if things get better you'll benefit with the rest of us."

Bannerman had been in the newspaper business too long to begin doing anything else; he was nearly sixty. So he said, "O. K., Ed." And, on an old typewriter in the city room he wrote 1,500 words on the current stage offerings, including a tribute to his much-respected and loved predecessor. His stuff, as Allen said, never had been better; it improved.

The Bannermans, with an income reduced to a third, moved to a cheaper apartment. The three children were married; two were not liabilities, but Bannerman had always had to take care of Grace and her husband, who seemed never to get into a paying business. On the contrary, Bannerman in seven years had lent him $11,000, which he never would get back, and supported the couple.

Yet the Courier job was better than nothing, which had ghostily stared at him for an interminable week, and except for the money it was a happy and important job. But after a year of it Allen sent for him. "Bob," he said, "I told you that if things got better, we'd see that you'd be the first to benefit. Well, they're worse." "They're better in my department," said Bannerman. "I know that theater advertising has almost doubled in a year." "There has been a slight increase in that department," said Allen, "but it's the only one. And we've got to play ball together. Or else," said Allen; "we don't want to stand in your way if you think you can do better elsewhere." So Bannerman, disheartened at what he knew for injustice and despotism—for he knew that Allen knew that he couldn't get another dramatic job, regardless of his ability—took the 20 per cent cut offered. It took the lightness and the bite out of his stuff; for a strong sense of futility overcame him, knowing that for years his work had been not only brilliant but also conscientious. He tried not to let the "What's-the-use?" feeling affect his work; it did affect it.

"I'm afraid," said Allen, sending for him again, after a few preliminaries, "we'll have to make a change in the department. Some of the managers have been complaining, and I'm afraid your heart isn't in it any more." "Whose would be," he asked, "after being chiseled down to a measly salary? You folks ought to be ashamed to look me in the face." "See here, Bob, that's no way to talk," said Allen. "We gave you the job because we were sorry for you, and we're giving young Stevenson a try at it now. Of course, we'll see that you get a month's salary. Got your Sunday piece up?" "Yes," said Bannerman, and walked out, indignant, dejected. He had $20 in his pocket, his assets after thirty-two years of successful journalism. He went to Webb's, the saloon across the street, the meeting-place of the town's solvent, for a day at any rate, newspapermen. Six or seven men greeted him warmly. "Well, well," was the burden of their hails, "Glad to see you, Bob. Don't remember ever seeing you in here. Drink?" So back and forth the treating went. Five hours later, with 75 cents in his pocket, and more drinks than he had had in the entire past decade, he took a cab home—50 cents, tip included.

It was past midnight; Mrs. Bannerman was asleep; she went to bed early on nights she didn't go to the theater with Bannerman. Bannerman sank into bed, drunk, tired, full of hatred for Allen, the Courier, the whole newspaper business that he had given his life to, as indeed it had given life to him; it was his life, and he looked at it, and it was no good.

At noon Mrs. Bannerman opened his door quietly, slowly. Still asleep. She closed the door, went to the kitchen and scrambled an egg for her lunch, washed the dish and the pan, and went back to the sleeper. Still asleep. "Robert," she called. She went to him and touched him gently. She shook him, first a little, then vigorously. No response. She felt his face; it was cold.

"Hello," said Mrs. Bannerman, "I want Mr. Edgar Allen, the editor." "He's in an editorial conference," said his secretary. "I don't care what he's in or out of," said Mrs. Bannerman, "tell him it's important news about Bob Bannerman." The switch to the conference room was made. "This is Mrs. Bannerman," she said. "Yes, Mrs. Bannerman," said Allen, dreading a talk with a woman whose husband had been fired. Usually he refused to talk to them. "And how are you?" "I'm just fine," she said. "Listen. Bob died in his sleep last night. He came in late, and I didn't see him till I found him. I thought you ought to know so as to get somebody to do the opening tonight."

"Thank you," said Allen, relieved, and feeling the guiltiest he had felt since he had been a boy. "Can we do anything? For you, I mean. You must know how we all feel, Mrs. Bannerman." But there was no response. Mrs. Bannerman, having done her duty as a reporter to her husband, had hung up.

Allen spoke to the other editorial writers. "Bob Bannerman died in his sleep last night. I'll tell the city desk to send somebody up to get a good obit. I'll do the editorial myself."

Allen went to his office and closed the door. "Anybody telephones," he told his secretary in an adjacent cubicle, "I'm not in."

Allen worked for a long time; he wrote in pencil and threw sheet after sheet away. He walked to the city room and by discreet inquiry learned that nobody but himself knew that Bannerman had lost his job. Allen, putting himself in Bannerman's place, knew that he wouldn't have told his wife, not while he still had a dollar.

After a considerable time Allen finished. Marking it "brev edit turn rule," he sent it to the composing room. Then he put on his hat, told Miss Bernard that he wouldn't be back, and went directly home. "You're home early," said Mrs. Allen. "I felt a little tired," said Allen.

And in next morning's Courier appeared:

ROBERT BANNERMAN

In the ineffably sad and untimely death of Robert Bannerman the Courier loses not only a close and warm friend but as loyal and unsparing an associate as any newspaper possibly could have. The Courier was Bob Bannerman's first and, as it turned out to be, his last love. Thirty-two years ago he came here as a reporter; he became, through sheer ability that often mounted to genius, dramatic critic, and save for a few years on the late Gazette, he was our dramatic critic to the end. When the Gazette came to an end, the Courier hailed him back home with joy, for the Courier was home to him.

As a critic there was nobody to approach him; in style, in the sanity of his views, and in the ripeness of his experience. He was held in deep affection by all his coworkers, and the stage—actors, playwrights, and managers—respected his critiques and enjoyed his light touch, though his deep sense of justice often caused him, so high were his standards, to be bitter.

A Bannermanless Courier, a Bannermanless first night, and a Bannermanless world are hard to imagine.

Bob, *ave atque vale!*

* * *

AN INTERVIEW WITH FRANK SULLIVAN

CONNING TOWER—What magazine do you write for?

SULLIVAN—The New Yorker, the sophisticated weekly.

C. T.—Do you get up early?

S.—Sometimes I rise at the crack of dawn.

C. T.—Do you work late?

S.—I burn the midnight oil, in the wee sma' hours.

C. T.—Where have you been?

S.—I have been spending the heated term at the Spa.

C. T.—Was it fun?

S.—Loads. I am an ardent devotee of the Sport of Kings.

C. T.—No athletics?

S.—I often indulged in the Royal and Ancient Game.

C. T.—Any good at it?

S.—I just play at it—a duffer.

C. T.—What did you enjoy most about it?

S.—The shower after the game was the best part.

C. T.—Do you take yourself seriously?

S.—No. Thank Heaven, I have the American sense of humor.

C. T.—What is that?

S.—The national trait. It is the saving grace.

C. T.—What do you save it for?

S.—I save it for a rainy day.

C. T.—What do most Americans do with theirs?

S.—They put it away and forget about it.

* * *

This student of income taxation is worried. "A taxpayer," the ruling says, "who supports in his home his minor children over whom he exercises family control is classified as the head of a family." To the Collector of Internal Revenue, Hartford, Conn.: Is it all right if that control is wavering, and if sometimes the control is, as you might say, on the other foot?

* * *

That it is fantastic to suggest that the United States is in any danger of attacks from Europe, Asia, or Africa we believe, with Col. Robert R. McCormick. It is a fantastic world, however, in which it was fantastic, not so long ago, to think that one humorless man could enslave his own people, and the people of so many other nations that it is beginning to be horrible to enumerate them. Even an attack by a foreign nation on the United States would be not more fantastic than the realistic history of the past three years.

* * *

"No man can be well dressed," observes Mrs. Carmel Snow, "who allows his wife to select his clothing." Nonsense. Wives are singularly unobservant about their husband's clothing. A man has a four-year old suit pressed, and his wife says, "That's a nice new suit. Guess whom I had lunch with today."

* * *

Mrs. Snow says that American men are not well dressed, and that they are the "blue-gray shadow timidly following in the wake of their wives." It is not the women who cause men to be conservative, timid dressers; it is other men. When a man's apparel—suit, necktie, shirt—goes to the gay side, women are likely to say, "What a lovely necktie!" Men jeer, whistle, and hoot.

* * *

It is our opinion that Mr. Willkie stood up exceedingly well under the long testimony that he gave on Tuesday. But his "Oh, that was campaign oratory" makes us indignant; indignant that there should be a hatchet to bury. Why campaign oratory should be something that should be spoken of as something said "in the heat of the campaign" we don't see, and we never did see. Why a man should say in effect "I hate that man, and if he is elected I am sorry for the country," and then say "Of course, I didn't mean it literally" we don't understand.

* * *

It is Mr. Westbrook Pegler's notion that Mrs. Roosevelt should specify what charities she gives her radio money to. She does so specify, but not to Mr. Pegler nor to us, neither of whose business it is. Hereafter, Mrs. R., please make your income tax report and mail it to Mr. Pegler, and not to the Collector of Internal Revenue.

* * *

Whether it is the impatience of youth or the testiness of senescence we are too impatient to ascertain. But we confess to a growing impatience with book reviewers. We should like to see one good critical piece upon verbosity. Does the critic who reviews at least five or six books a week never feel that a book is too long? Does he never assail a publisher for encouraging authors to write long books? What provoked this paragraph was the Little, Brown advertisement of "Oliver Wiswell" as "this great 836-page masterpiece." Of course, "Delilah" is a curtain-raiser of only 495 pages, and "Long Meadows" comes to its end on page 656. Negley Farson's "Behind God's Back" is only 555 pages; but

John Cowper Powys's "Owen Glendower" gallops along through 938 pages; we recall one night in January when we turned out the light at page 18, and somehow we don't know yet how page 19 *et seq.* turned out.

That animadversion upon length for length's sake was getting a little wordy.

Of course, it is not necessary for a reviewer to read every word of a book to write a highly competent appraisal of it. But we wish some reviewer—Mr. Hansen, Mr. Fadiman, Mr. Gannett, or Mr. Prescott—would read every word of one of these books that give more, if not better, words for the money. Call the author by name, and show him why his book is too long.

* * *

It is, many a broadcaster evidently contends, a free country, and he doesn't know whom can make him join the English Speaking Union, which acks like it had athawrity.

* * *

There was a time, a time forever gone—ah, me!—when Greenland was something that things were colder than, and the Axis was something that the world revolved upon instead of turned against.

* * *

IF I OWNED A NEWSPAPER

If I owned a newspaper is not so hypothetical as it sounds. I owned a part of a newspaper—The New York Evening Mail, The New York Tribune, The New York World and The New York Herald Tribune—for thirty-three years. In each of these papers I ran a column—not a weekly or tri-weekly department of varying length, but a daily column one column long. I could say, and did say, what I liked about anything or everybody, as much or as little. In all those years no owner or editor ever asked me to write this or not to write that, or to devote more space to this or less to that.

I except a few things: My first editor, W. K. McKay of The Chicago Journal, told me not to use the word "crooks." "Most of our advertisers are," he said, "and they're sensitive about it." On The Tribune I wrote a paragraph about Charles W. Morse. Morse, financier and steamship owner, was convicted of misapplication of funds owing to the failure of the New Amsterdam Bank. He entered the Federal Penitentiary at Atlanta in January, 1910; he was pardoned two years later by President Taft, his physicians and attorneys convincing that soft-hearted executive that the state of Morse's health would not give him much longer to live. He died in 1933. I wrote a lot of indignant and, to my notion, satirical paragraphs, mostly to the effect that the unmoneyed crooks stayed in prison.

One paragraph ran: "Mr. Charles W. Morse, of Atlanta and New York, came back from Europe yesterday in good health and spirits. Lupo the Wolf, of New York and Atlanta, was reported in good health," and another: "We hope that Mr. Leo M. Frank, of Atlanta, saw and was cheered by the picture, published Saturday, of Mr. Charles W. Morse as he was about to sail for Bermuda." That, or something else, caused Morse to remove the advertisement of his steamship lines from The Tribune. "That paragraph cost us $4000," Mr. G. V. Rogers, the business manager, told me. "Try to make 'em a little cheaper." Mr. Rogers was good-natured, especially as The Tribune in 1914, when the paragraphs appeared, could not afford to throw $4,000 out of the window.

Later, in 1921, P. F. Collier and Son ran a full-page Sunday advertisement of the Five Foot Shelf. I kidded the priggishness of it; the notion that the bookworm was a fascinator. My stuff was nearly a column long, and—I read it the other day, sixteen years after publication, and knew it for one of my few good pieces—I received this letter:

March 30, 1921.

Mr. Adams:

I want to thank you for "The Art of Fascinating," which you ran in yesterday's column.

It has only cost us about $12,000 in the first 24 hours.

My congratulations on your effective work.

G. V. R.

But even then I was not asked to lay off advertisers.

Those were the exceptions from 1903 to 1921. In 1928 for The World, I wrote a paragraph quoting an advertisement: "Advertising English by Saks-Fifth Avenue: 'The Last Word . . . even for we moderns.'" And a day or two later I wrote: "Not to be outdone by Saks-Fifth Avenue, Franklin Simon and Company advertised: 'Hats for She Who Wears the Largest Head Size.'" It is true that many an advertiser thanked me for printing such slips in English, but Mr. Florence D. White, business manager of The World, wrote this memorandum to Mr. H. B. Swope, the executive editor:

Why not *order* F. P. A. to ignore advertising copy on his criticisms? He has the whole Book World to shoot at.

Why not, at the same time, order him to stop advertising stores in his column?

Do you think these uncalled-for slaps at the advertising managers of Saks & Co. and Franklin Simon & Co. renders the work of Mr. Merrill's department any easier in going up against wounded pride?

No other newspaper in the country would stand for this deviltry of an employee.

Why do we?

Mr. Swope told Mr. White that he thought a number of advertisers liked to be criticized. "They like to get their names in print that, after all, is not particularly critical." Swope, however, suggested that I leave out the criticism of advertisers. "There has been no holler," he added. "But, with all Literature, Drama and the other Arts—with all of which you are familiar—from which you can make a selection of subject, why waste time on advertising writers." Incidentally, Mr. White thought that The World always overpaid Heywood Broun and me, regardless of our salaries; as far as I know, Swope always stood up for us against White.

Naturally, my experiences as a newspaper writer would influence my ownership of a mythical newspaper. These are some of the things that I would do:

I would run it as a morning tabloid. The news stories would begin on page 1, and if long enough would be continued on page 2; I would avoid the big "jumps" prevalent in most newspapers. Except in rare instances news would be unaccompanied by pictures. The paper would be a daily, the Sunday edition being no more voluminous than the other six issues.

I would have no comics, or comic strips.

I would have no syndicated features. If you wanted to read my Broun or Thompson or Winchell—maybe I wouldn't employ any of them—you would have to buy my paper; my writers wouldn't be under the pressure, subtle or definite, of having to make their stuff just as readable—or as mediocre—in Eastport, Maine, as in Seattle, Washington, the same morning.

My paper would cost five cents a copy so that circulation and distribution would at least pay for themselves. A newspaper selling at two cents does not pay the expenses of composition, ink, paper, distribution and personnel; therefore the importance of advertising is overemphasized.

Advertisers would have no influence on the editorial department and there would be no such thing as a b. o. m., which, as all my former buddies on city staffs know, is Business Office Must. Nor would I attack an advertiser in or out of the paper merely to exhibit my paper's courage and independence.

I would be independent politically. By independent I mean independent, and not (Ind. Rep.) or (Ind. Dem.).

I would pay excellent salaries, as a minimum. And I should issue to the staff quarterly statements of profits and losses. There would be salary revisions once a year, based upon the annual statement. If the paper lost money, nobody would be cut below the minimum; if the paper showed a profit, salaries would be adjusted proportionally—not on the bonus system, but throughout the year.

I would run at most two editorials, oftener one. This is the New York Daily News's way, and a good way, too. I would print the names of the editorial writers, and maybe I would have each editorial signed.

It is absurd to say that I would run an honest paper, or one characterized by good taste. Those are matters of definition. My honesty is somebody else's quixotism, or compromise; my good taste is somebody else's Nice Nellie-ism, or vulgarity.

I would run crime stories when the news demanded their printing.

My sport department would not be topheavy. That is, it would not specialize in fights, baseball and racing at the expense of golf and tennis and other amateur sports. I would eliminate ballyhoo—whipping up interest in a fight, or a football or baseball game. I would print attendance figures only when the record was official. The overestimation of crowds by sport writers infuriates me, and while it is supposed to arouse so much interest that everybody will want to go, it more often has the effect of keeping people away. Besides, many of the advance estimates are made in order to do a favor to some manager whose business will be increased by such publicity.

I would have an exchange editor who read the out-of-town papers mostly for the purpose of finding some bushel-hid talent.

Mr. Rollin Kirby tells me that if he owned a newspaper he would immediately hire The London Evening Standard's cartoonist, David Low. If he wouldn't come, I would get Kirby or The Baltimore Sun's Edmund Duffy. My cartoonist could pick his subject; it could be political, social, literary or anything else he might choose.

I would try to get the best foreign correspondents, realizing how many countries there are that would throw them out if they told the truth, and that in most nations truth-telling dries up the sources of news.

I would charge a high rate of advertising, believing that advertising space is proportional; that if the largest advertisement were two columns instead of two pages, a half-column would be a big display.

I would print no Society News, as such.

I would keep editorial bias, not only from news stories, but also from headlines. Most papers will tell you that this is what they do; The New York Times is the least frequent offender in stories and headlines. Most other newspapers offend by condoning the political or other prejudices of the owner. A copyreader consciously or unconsciously wants to please the boss. He writes "Hoover Defies New Deal" or "Roosevelt's Court plan Wise, Say Senators." All this could be obviated by a vigilant and ethical managing editor. He should tell the copydesk that the paper wants headlines to be unprejudiced; and whenever a biased headline appears, the copyreader should be told that it violates the principle— my principle, anyway—of newspaper ethics.

I would spend at least six or seven hours a day in my office. I would know every member of the editorial and business staffs, to any of whom I would be easily accessible.

Every member of the staff would read most of his paper every day. At intervals I would have brief quizzes on matters connected with current news events.

Obviously, my theatre, music and book-review departments would be as editorial as good criticism should be.

I would get out the kind of newspaper that I, as a reader, would like to read, as opposed to a fictitious reading public whose wants I uncannily knew. I might soon lose even my unlimited money, but I would not, at any rate, be like Kin Hubbard's friend, Tilford Moots, who "wuz over t' th' Henryville poor farm th' other day t' see an ole friend o' his thet used t' publish a newspaper thet pleased ever'buddy."

* * *

THE ART OF FASCINATING

"Which of these two men," the advertisement demands, "has learned the secret of fifteen minutes a day?" The advertisement is P. F. Collier & Son Company's.

Gaze on the picture. A beautiful young woman is seated, between two men, at a table. Coffee has been served; and, though nobody is smoking, indications are that a pleasant time is being had. But, soft! Not by all. Beaming upon the young man to her right with a warm approval that another spark would make into candescent admiration and worship, the young woman, her lips slightly parted, sits; the young man at her right obviously is talking to her; the young man at her left, with what we take to be an envious look, observes his rival. He appears to be biting his nails, registering jealousy. He looks not unlike the old pictures we used to see in the patent medicine advertisement labeled we believe, General Debility. So much for the picture.

"Here," continues the advertisement, "are two men, equally good looking, equally well dressed. You see such men at every social gathering. One of them can talk of nothing beyond the mere day's news. The other brings to every subject a wealth of side-light and illustration that makes him listened to eagerly. He talks like a man who has traveled widely, though his only travels are a business man's trips. He knows something of history and biography, of the work of great scientists, and the writings of philosophers, poets, and dramatists."

"The answer," the advertisement goes on—but you know what it says. You know that it says you may have this man's Success for the asking; that if you became a bookworm that burrowed fifteen whole minutes a day in your books—the Five-Foot Shelf, to be precise—Beauty would beam upon you, too; you, too, would be a Masterful Man, a Conquering Hero.

Remote be it from us to throw doubt upon the effect of an advertisement. Why, some of our best friends are advertisers, and we wouldn't offend one of them for the solar system with Betelguese thrown in. But candor compels the admission that our answer to the question quoted in the first sentence of this piece was wrong. In a word, we thought the discomfited looking man was the bookworm. To us he looked as though he were thinking, "How is it possible for that girl to listen to that incessant, egotistic piffle? She appears interested. Is she? I've seen 'em pretend to be fascinated by what men were saying, when all the time their little brains—if any—were thinking of something else. I wish I could get away and get back to my Five-Foot Shelf. This is a sad evening. Won't he ever stop?

What the advertisement wants you to think he is saying is, "A murrain on his fatal gift of fascination! Him with his fine words and his book learning! I wish I had not squandered my time. How lightly, yet how confidently, he mentions Cavour, Columbus, Darwin, Epictetus, Emerson, Euripides! And next week, curse his acquisitiveness, he will have read up to F, perhaps G!"

And also, according to the advertisement, the Cultured (self) young man is speaking of just such things; and Beauty, enraptured, marvels that one head, handsome though it be, can hold all that knowledge.

But our interpretation of the picture is this: It looks to us, as has been said, as if the disgruntled young man were the tome-hound. And, despairing of leading the talk to matters of history and biography, etc., he is listening to the handsome young man say to the Fairest of Her Sex, "And I said to him, 'Say, Mr. Swope, who do you think you're talkin' to?' And I took my hat and walked out and left him flat. I'm as good as he is. . . . Say, what say to going over to Montmartre or the Palais Royal and having a couple of dances or six?"

"I'd *love* to," says Beauty, "If Mr.—now—Gazish will excuse us."

"Oh," the bookworm—according to our interpretation, not to Collier's—would say "Certainly. Sure. That's all right. I ought to be going home anyway."

That's what would have happened. We know. As Frank Bacon used to say, we were a bookworm ourself once.

* * *

THE CLANG OF THE HITLER BELL

After Gilbert

'Twas in a town I can't recall,
　Whether Omsk or Ispahan,
That I met one week a terribly sleek
　And sleekly terrible man.

His little mustache was silly and short,
　And silly and short was he,
And I heard this guy that I spoke of cry,
　In a tone that was off the key:

"Oh, I am a boss and a Fuehrer bold,
　And the Czechoslovak nurse,
The Queen of the May and the U. S. A.,
　And the King of the Universe."

And he shook his fists and he tore his hair,
　And never a smile smole he,
And I said, "Oh, hell, go on and tell
　How you can possibly be

At once a boss and a Fuehrer bold,
　And the Czechoslovak nurse,
The Queen of the May and the U. S. A.,
　And the King of the Universe."

Then he takes a trip to the microphone,
　And bellers and yells and hollers,
And to listening folk he also spoke
　Substantially as follers:

"There was me and the boss and the Fuehrer bold,
　And the Czechoslovak nurse,

The Queen of the May and the U. S. A.,
   And the King of the Universe."

And he says, "I'll do what I bloody choose,
   And nobody says me nay,
And I hate the Catholics and the Jews,
   And the whole of the U. S. A.

"And I gobbled the Czech, and I seared his soul,
   And I swallowed the land and sea,
The Briton, the Gaul, the Russ, the Pole,
   And nobody's left but me.

"And I never grin, and I never smile,
   And I never larf nor play,
But I scream and croak, and a single-joke
   I have—which is to say:

"Oh, I am a boss and a Fuehrer bold,
   And the Czechoslovak nurse,
The Queen of the May and U. S. A.,
   And the King of the Universe."

* * *

This column is in warm accord with Mr. Jonathan Daniels, editor of the Raleigh News and Observer, who says that the most dangerous threat to newspapers today is giving the people the news they want to receive. We qualify it. Our feeling is that the dangerous threat is the editor or publisher who runs his paper in the mistaken notion of pleasing all his readers. Again we quote one of our favorite lines from Kin Hubbard, which is capsule history of journalism: "Tilford Moots wuz over t' th' Henryville poor farm th' other day t' see an ole friend o' his thet used t' publish a newspaper thet pleased ever'buddy."

* * *

The Nazi Government has decreed the suppression of all Catholic publications in the Reich, and the New York Times observes that it can "only arouse a new wave of resentment the world over." One trouble with the non-Nazi world is that such things no longer arouse a wave of resentment; the world is so inured to that sort of intolerance and injustice— for which apathy the radio and the newspapers are not blameless—that such things have to be conspicuous to cause a ripple.

For the radio commenters use too many italics of speech, and the newspapers use too many daily 8-column streamers. So when there is something unusually important to say the coins of emphasis are worn thin. It is like continuous profanity; when the user wants to be stressful he has no way to convey his irritation, indignation, or outright anger. Tut!

* * *

Father is the fellow who gives the kids five dollars so that they can give him a dollar's worth of candy, and four five-cent cigars.

* * *

"Bartlett pears of fine flavor and solid flesh," observes Miss Jane Holt in the Times, "are said to be ideal for stuffing with cream cheese and nuts for a warm-weather fruit salad dessert." Said by whom? Because any lily-painter that spoils pears, or any other fruit, by the addition of cream cheese and nuts, or tries to make a salad of a self-respecting fruit, has us to fight. Those are the same kitchen-meddlers who put sugar on tomatoes, and cinnamon and cloves in pies. . . . By the way, next time we see anybody put brown gravy on cold roast beef, the second thing we do will be to hand ourself over to the police.

* * *

PRAYER OF MOTHERS

O God of War, thy wrinkled brow
I prithee smooth, and smooth it now
For war is a terrible tale to tell
For men—but oh, for mothers, hell.
Yet if the direful fates decree
For war, I ask but this of thee
Let it come now, but oh, be done
While yet too youthful is my son.

* * *

"MY DAY"

(Written in accordance with a promise made to chronicle an ordinary day, as Mr. A. A. Schechter did in "I Live on Air.")

Woke at 5:35, probably because of melted snow from the roof dripping on my window sill. Read "My Father Was an Editor," by Joshua K. Bolles of New Milford.

Rose at 6:45, went downstairs and turned on the heat, went upstairs and closed Timmy's window. Shaved, bathed, and dressed. Went to breakfast, with Puffy and Jack. Drove the 1932 Franklin to the station, stopping on Main Street for 10 gallons of gasoline, $1.48. Lots of ice and snow at parking place, so I barely made the 8:16, grabbing N. Y. Times, N. Y. Herald Tribune, and Bridgeport Telegram, putting 9c on cuff. Read papers, and finished H. T. X-word puzzle between Fordham and 125th Street. Stood up in subway to Wall Street.

Had income tax schedule signature notarized. What did I do with the income?

Opened mail. Put one or two pieces aside to use in case of emergency. I ought to know better. Don't print one in a hundred that I do that with.

Letter marked personal from S. A. Scheier, enclosing circular offering me The Gag File for $100. Jokes to use in my work.

Letter from a woman asking me not to use her name in printing "the following" in my Herald Tribune column.

Miss Barbara Durham wonders "if you would send some material on your life in the newspaper business." Deadline April 15. "Send all possible information about your life." No stamp encl.

Hanford L. Hardin wants to know "the author of the attached poem 'Myself.'" Told him I never had heard of it. Why don't people look things up for themselves?

A boy from Royal Oak, Mich., wants me to reprint a poem which was printed in his school publication. His English professor [sic] thought it was quite good. No accounting for tastes, as the woman said when somebody told her her son was wanted by the police.

Looked at a proof, and saw that I had said that "Trumpets of Jubilee" had been written by Constance Lindsay Skinner. Got to thinking. Went downstairs again, and looked in "Who's Who in America." Should have said Constance Mayfield Rourke. Made the correction.

Mrs. G. C. Blalock, West Lafayette, Ind., says that the Literature Section of the Purdue Women's Club "expect to put on a program dealing with various phases of humor in modern Literature." Wants to know whether I issue a year book. Told her no. Says she likes Mr. Kiernan [sic].

Postal card writer "would appreciate very much if you could supply necessary information whereby I may obtain the words of a poem I have entirely forgotten. It starts, as follows—St. Peter stood at the golden gate with a solemn mien & air sedate, when up to the top of the golden stairs a man & woman ascended there." Never heard of it, but I'll bet that it's in one of those 100-Recitations books.

Woman calls and wants to know my address. I ask why. Says she has a poem she would like to send to The Coning [*sic*] Tower. Tell her to send it care of the Wichita Beacon. Says "I thought if I sent it to the N'Yawk Post it would be all right." Tell her maybe that would save a little time, at that.

Ten poems, full of prosy platitudes and cliches, attacking Senator Wheeler.

Wrote a few paragraphs and some couplets.

Got a copy of the Thorndike Century Senior Dictionary, with my name on the cover. Scott, Foresman and Company, the publishers, want to know what I think of it. Seems all right, from A, the first letter of the alphabet to zyme, any ferment, virus, etc., that causes an infectious disease. Live and learn, as if it hadn't been that they wanted to know what I thought, I never should have known about zyme. Maybe the next time I see something of the kind in a certain newspaper I'll credit to the New York Zymes. Maybe not.

Spent some time in the composing room, making up. Had a three-line paragraph overset.

Telephone, asking me to make a speech. Say "I don't speak."

Telephone, asking for Deems Taylor's address. Who wants it? A personal friend. Columbia Broadcasting System. "Isn't he on one of the newspapers?" What a personal friend! Why didn't I tell her that he's on the New York World?

Rollin Kirby comes in and wants to know how long it will take me to finish. Say not long if he'll keep his trap shut. If a man keeps his trap shut the world will beat a path to his door. Let him read my copy of Police Gazette; says "Don't hurry. Oh, boy!"

Hurry to subway. Can't understand why people walk in triple file on one of the narrowest sidewalks in town. Yes, I can. People are inconsiderate. Just miss subway train. Get to Grand Central in time for 5:31. Drive home, and have supper with Tat and Tim.

Went to PTA meeting at school, Tim being inducted in Boy Scouts, the first troop ever in our town. Got home, and was firm about Tim going right to bed. Showed him that I was in bed, which I was.

* * *

TO A COQUETTE

Quis multa gracilis te puer in rosa . . .
—Horace: Odes. Book I.

What graceful youth, perfumed and slender,
Bids you, O Pyrrha, to surrender,
Embracing you for half an hour
Within the rose-encrusted bower?

Alas! how often will this youth
Sadden at seas no longer smooth!
And oh! how frequently he'll wonder
At waters rough with dark and thunder!

Doomed are the lads who when they meet
You think that you are honey-sweet;
As far as I'm concerned I'm through
With polyandrous girls like you.

* * *

DR. SPENCER'S CLOCK

It isn't as though ours were a clockless house. We are clock poor. My wife is a glutton for clocks. In the days when a nickel was chicken feed, and not either carfare or something you saved by walking; in the days when, if your stock increased a thousand dollars a day the headline was "Market in Doldrums;" in those days my wife bought clocks. She bought them and forgot about them. So we have a beautiful French clock in the bedroom. It is on the mantelpiece, and it says 9:35. The dining-room clock's hands are at 10:18. One that my wife bought in Camden, Maine, as something pre-Revolutionary, and is dated 1862 Ansonia Conn., she carried in her arms from Camden to Westport, Conn.—that is in the living-room, and says 11:10, and it is my favorite, because it is the only clock we have that looks as though it went, and visitors take a look and say, "Oh, it's late. You good people must be tired. Besides, we have to go," and there isn't one visitor in ten I feel like telling the truth to. None of these clocks, since my wife bid, furiously and alas! successfully, for them at auctions, ever has ticked ten minutes.

My wristwatch has a luminous dial, but I never look at it at night. For I not only don't get enough sleep, but I worry about not getting enough, too. All insomniacs do that, till we don't sleep because we worry about it and we worry because we don't sleep. I think of myself, in my wakeful moments of acute self-pity, as Sisyphus rolling a snowball uphill. The reason I don't look at my watch is that I do not want to know what time it is. If I found that I hadn't got to sleep till 4 o'clock and knew that I had to get up at 7:30, I wouldn't sleep anything like three and a half hours. I'd hurry so to get it that my heart would pound and shake the bed, and then I'd be lucky to get one hour. Then I'd worry because I would fear the consequences of sleeplessness, chief among them being the impairment of my abilities. I don't always have to get up at 7:30, but try sleeping in my bed later than that, with the patter of little feet—eight—in the room above, at the time of four breakfasts.

Now next door live the Dr. Spencers. Who lives in the room

contiguous to my bedde's hedde I don't know; not in seven years have I heard a voice or other human sound in that room. But it has a clock. I can't hear it tick, but I can and do hear it strike. Say I go to bed at 10:01, and read till 10:20. I fall asleep at 10:25, and then I hear the clock next door strike once. Only the sleepless know what it means to wonder whether it is 1 o'clock, 10:30, or 3:30. Pride keeps me from looking at my watch. But what makes the nights white, what makes me wish that the Spencers would either stop the clock or put it in a more remote room is this: I awake, and hear that strike. If it happens to be 3:00, or any other hour, that is all right. I go right to slumberland. But if the strike is one, I lie there waiting for the next. By the time it comes—say 4 or 5—I am vigilance's own. No more sleep for me. I am indignant at the clock, and angry at myself for letting a thing like that distress me. So I hear them all—5:30, 6:30, and 7. I fool the clock by getting up at 7:25.

But this is child's play. Man's work comes at 12:30, for there is no strike you can be certain of till 2 o'clock.

Well, I met Dr. Spencer this morning in front of the house. "How are you?" he said. "All right," I said. "You look a little tired," he said. "I was up late last night," I said, "writing a little article."

* * *

THE COWARD POET

I've tried and sweated, sweated and tried,
Yet far the cry, the gap how wide
From what I meant to what I've said,
From living thoughts to phrases dead,
From what I feel to what I say
To make a verbal holiday;
Nor have I had at any time

Courage to write except in rhyme,
Nor bravery to be unrefined,
For mine is but a little mind
That ties itself to a tiny art
Lest it should show a beating heart;
And so to facts I sham devotion
Lest I exhibit my emotion.

Forgive me for my rhyming prose,
And for the limits I impose
Upon my heart, upon my pen,
And curse me for a coward.

                           Amen.

Index of Titles

INDEX OF TITLES